Homes
of Kings

The Grand Tour

Homes of Kings

Flavio Conti

Translated by: Patrick Creagh

HBJ Press
New York

HBJ Press

President, Robert J. George

Publisher, Giles Kemp

Vice President, Richard S. Perkins, Jr.

Managing Director, Valerie S. Hopkins

Text Director, Marcia Heath

Text Editors: Elizabeth R. DeWitt, Karen E.
  English, Carolyn Hall, Peggy Wagner,
  Gregory Weed

Editorial Staff: Betsie Brownell, Karen Fraser,
  Ann McGrath, Nancy Knoblock, Janet
  Schotta

Project Coordinator, Linda S. Behrens

Architectural Consultant, Dennis J. DeWitt

Project Consultant, Ann S. Moore

Design Implementation, Designworks

Rizzoli Editore

Authors of the Italian Edition: Jiri Burian, Dr.
  Flavio Conti, Henri Stierlin, Jersy
  Szablowski, Dr. Gian Maria Tabarelli

Idea and Realization, Harry C. Lindinger

General Supervisor, Luigi U. Re

Graphic Designer, Gerry Valsecchi

Coordinator, Vilma Maggioni

Editorial Supervisor, Gianfranco Malafarina

Research Organizer, Germano Facetti

U.S. Edition Coordinator, Natalie Danesi
  Murray

Photography Credits:

*Agencija Autorska-Andrulewicz, Siemaszko, Szuster,
Wierzla:* all pictures from pp. 105–116 / *Aerofilm:* pp.
122–123 / *C.E.D.R.I.:* pp. 10–11 / *Dilia-Neubert:* pictures
on pp. 92–93, 94 top, 95 top, all pictures on pp.
153–164 / *Giraudon:* p. 16 bottom left and right, 17 bottom
left, 18 top left, center left, bottom left, 19 top & bottom,
21 top left & right, 25 bottom, 26 top, 31 top / *Hervé:* p.
141 top & bottom, 143 bottom, 145 top left, 146
top / *Hirmer:* p. 144, p. 147 all pictures / *Interfoto F.
Rausch:* p. 140 top, pp. 58–59 / *Magnum:* pp.
138–139 / *Magnum-Barbey:* p. 44 top right, 49
bottom / *Magnum-Burri:* p. 46 top, 48 top & bottom, 49
top, p. 52 / *Magnum-Capa:* p. 80 top / *Magnum-Davidson:*
p. 96 / *Magnum-Lessing:* pp. 74–75, 76 top, 77, 78, 146
bottom / *Magnum-Manos:* p. 81 top /. *Magnum-Riboud:*
pp. 41–43, 44 top left, 44 bottom left & right, 45, 46
bottom, 47 top, 47 bottom left & right, 50
top / *Magnum-Rowan:* p. 79 top / *Novosti:* pp. 73, 76
bottom left & right, 78 top, 81 bottom, 82–87, all pictures
on pp. 89–91, 94 bottom, 95 bottom left, middle &
right / *Publifoto:* pp. 78 bottom, 79 bottom, 80
bottom / *Rizzoli:* p. 9, 12 bottom, 13, 16 top & bottom
left, 17 top right, center right & bottom right, 20, 21
bottom left, middle & bottom right, 24, 25 top left & right,
26 bottom, 27, 28, 30, 31 bottom left & right, 32, 121, 126
top, 132 / *Scala:* pp. 12 top, 14–15, 22–23, 29 / *Sheridan:*
pp. 124–125, p. 126 bottom, all pictures on pp. 127–131,
137, 140 bottom, 141, 143 top, 145 top right & bottom,
148 / *Stierlin:* p. 57, all pictures on pp. 60–68 / *Verg:* pp.
46 middle, 50 bottom, 51.

Library of Congress Catalog Card Number: 77–882–45
ISBN: 0-15-003724-4

Printed in Italy

Contents

Preface

Homes of Kings

Throughout the centuries, the needs and desires—aesthetic, political, and utilitarian—of different civilizations and individuals have found expression in their architecture. From the earliest crude shelters to the magnificent palaces of the great rulers of history, the edifices constructed by man have not only satisfied his basic requirements, such as protection, but also expressed his wealth, sophistication, and status within the community.

Nowhere is this more evident than in the homes that kings have built for themselves, displaying their power and supremacy in elaborate palaces. The royal dwellings in *Homes of Kings* represent diverse cultures and span thousands of years. The tranquil beauty of the Forbidden City of Peking seems a world away from the enigmatic ruins at Knossos, and yet all eight palaces in this volume bear their own particular and eloquent testimony to the influence and sovereignty of their owners.

Not symbols of power alone, the palaces of kings reflect a basic human desire for immortality. Just as writers hope their ideas will last forever, kings and potentates build castles, cathedrals, and citadels to insure that they will not be forgotten by succeeding generations. Rulers have recorded their authority—and often their divine right—in wood and stone, and their

massive fortifications or beautiful palaces, which towered physically and symbolically over their subjects, have indeed survived centuries after their deaths.

In the course of time, however, these castles and palaces, once symbolizing the dominion of a royal and aristocratic elite, became a vital part of a national heritage. During the eighteenth century, the palace at Versailles epitomized the hated monarchy for the French people. Yet, during the Franco–Prussian War, nothing angered the nation more than the presence of the Germans in a place they regarded as a symbol of French pride: the Hall of Mirrors, with its frescoes glorifying French military victories.

Originally monuments to royal prestige, royal dwellings often serve commemorative functions, honoring national heroes, both historical and legendary. The Forbidden City of Peking now houses the remains of Mao Tse-tung, while Lenin's body lies in state alongside the Kremlin wall in Moscow.

The homes of kings are as varied as the rulers who built them and the cultures that inspired them. The Cretan labyrinthian palace at Knossos evolved from a civilization that never could have given rise to the feudal fortress of the Tower of London. The fortified citadels of the Wawel, the

Kremlin, and Hradčany; the Forbidden City of Peking; the landscaped palace at Versailles; and the ancient city of Persepolis are all unique products of a specific time and place. But despite their differences, each of these palaces was a stage upon which history was played out. Within their walls, tales of passion, of fame and intrigue, and of heroic victories and bitter losses have been enacted and later recorded by historians and sung by poets.

Shakespeare's tragedies dramatize the bloody history of the Tower of London, for centuries the setting of extraordinary scenes of intrigue and ambition. Here, Richard III, as portrayed by Shakespeare, is said to have murdered his young nephews and had the duke of Clarence drowned in a butt of malmsey. Here, the innocent Henry VI was killed at his prayers, and here, countless other great personages were imprisoned—some entering the Traitors' Gate from the Thames, never to return.

The palace of Knossos is also immortalized in legend. Capital of a flourishing Bronze Age culture, Knossos stands at the crossroads of history and mythology. Sir Arthur Evans's extensive excavations led him to believe that this was the palace of Minos. Today, the sunlit ruins call to mind the mythical architect Daedalus and his

Contents

winged flight with his son Icarus, the youths and maidens sacrificed to the Minotaur, and the love of Theseus and Ariadne.

The beautiful desert ruins at Persepolis were once the site of the flourishing ceremonial center of the vast and formidable Persian empire, finally felled by Alexander the Great. Today, all that remains of its cool halls and courtyards are revealing traces of buildings eroded by centuries of wind and sand.

The story of the Forbidden City of Peking is also the story of a proud and treasure-laden empire, which was unknown to Europeans before Marco Polo journeyed through the Orient and brought back fabulous tales of an advanced yet strange Chinese culture. Emperors and mandarins in Peking pursued refined pleasures and sometimes engaged in dark conspiracies. From within forbidding walls, they ruled their subjects with a sublime indifference.

The Kremlin in Moscow, so exotically oriental and romantic, has long symbolized Russia to Western eyes. Napoleon led his *grande armée* of half a million men across Russia to conquer it. Originally the seat of the feudal overlord of the city, it became the cradle of the czars, and its history is linked with the names of Ivan the Terrible, Peter the Great, Boris Godunov, and of course, Joseph Stalin.

The palace at Versailles was the creation of Louis XIV. "I am the State," declared the king, and he regarded the regal opulence of his palace as the embodiment and enhancement of his own self-proclaimed omnipotence. But the story of Versailles, like that of the Forbidden City and the Kremlin, does not stop with the glory of its great ruling monarchs. In later chapters in history, these bastions of regal power became the scenes of bloody revolutions. Today, they are used as official government buildings and museums.

The citadels of the Wawel in Krakow and Hradčany in Prague, although less well known in the West, also played dominant parts in the histories of their often troubled and oppressed nations. In 1794, the banner of rebellion was raised at the Wawel, the rallying signal for one of many ill-fated Polish insurrections. And at Hradčany, in 1618, the famous Defenestration of Prague—when the Bohemian Protestants simply threw the representatives of the Catholic emperor out a window—triggered the Thirty Years' War. Later, Rudolph of Hapsburg preferred Prague to Vienna and made it the capital of his empire.

The stories of these palaces also speak to us in other ways. Once centers of political, economic, and cultural life, they are also among the world's greatest treasuries of art and craftsmanship. The finest architects were commissioned to build them, and great painters, sculptors, landscape artists, and furniture designers were engaged to decorate and embellish them. Over the centuries, invaluable collections of artistic masterpieces were amassed, supplemented by gifts from foreign ambassadors and trophies from conquered lands. In these palaces can be seen crown jewels and other treasures of gold and silver, frescoes by great masters, sculptures of the Renaissance and of the grand siècle, and ornamental motifs of successive cultures and generations.

The palaces and castles of kings, and the priceless treasures housed within their walls, are expressions of a universal impulse—the impulse to build. John Ruskin, the Victorian cultural critic, once wrote: "I shall give him stones, and bricks and straw, chisels and trowels, and the ground and ask him to build." From the earliest times, men of vision have recognized the ways in which raw materials can be transformed into enduring monuments, which continue to provide us with one of the true keys to understanding fallen empires and the individuals who helped shape them.

Versailles,

France

Preceding page, a series of three courtyards—the Cour des Ministres, the Cour
Royale, and the Cour de Marbre—leads
from the entrance to the king's apartment.
From this center, two vast wings stretch out.
Beyond lie the gardens and the park. The
chapel juts out from the wing to the right
and is the only asymmetrically placed ele-
ment in the entire construction.

Above and left, the Cour des Ministres. In
the middle is the huge statue of Louis XIV
on horseback, which dates from the nineteenth century. This courtyard is the largest
in the palace and also the last to be built,
having been added by Mansart when the
court of Louis XIV was moved from Paris
to Versailles.

Above, a view of the courtyards from the roof of the palace.

Right, the Cour de Marbre, the innermost and oldest courtyard of the palace. Around it stood the original hunting lodge used by Louis XIII. The façades and the interior of the buildings around the courtyard were altered first by Le Vau and later by Mansart. The king's bedchamber, on the central axis of this courtyard, was at the center of the whole vast palace complex.

Below, the chateau seen from the entrance gates, with the series of three courtyards of decreasing size. To the right is the chapel.

Preceding page, the immense façade as seen across a basin in the park. Its final effect is one of unity, yet it was built in two successive phases, each different in spirit. The original design was by Le Vau, while Mansart added the wings and enclosed the arcaded loggia, which occupied the main floor of the central section.

Above, the Parterre du Midi, one of the vast geometric patterns of flower beds which distinguishes the palace gardens.

Left, two of the many urns that provide a transition between the architectural composition and the landscape gardening.

A series of views of the park showing the splendid achievement of the great landscape gardener Le Nôtre. Versailles created the popularity of the baroque "French garden," with its huge scale, expansive visual perspectives, and strategically placed fountains. The park is perhaps the dominant feature of Versailles, with its formal parterres, its great basins of water, its many lovely fountains, and the radial arrangement of avenues that unify the whole landscape. The Grand Trianon (center right) is one of two smaller palaces at Versailles.

Originally, the sculptural decoration of the parterres adjoining the palace was intended to be governed by a complex program based on the number four. There were to be groups representing the four continents, the four elements, the four times of the day. But then a simpler solution was found (left). Statues of reclining figures were designed to represent the rivers of France—each accompanied by cherubic figures. They were all carved by the royal artists Coysevox, Tuby, Regnaudin, Le Gros, and Le Hongre.

The great basins of water (right) are decorated with a vast number of sculptural motifs. The most famous is the central group on the Basin of Apollo (below), which represents the god's chariot drawn by four horses, surrounded by figures that suggest the sea. The eastern end of the Grand Canal where the Italian garden meets the park was a favorite spot of Louis XIV, and he frequently walked around the Basin of Apollo with all its playful fountains.

Apart from his work on the major buildings of the palace, Mansart was responsible for a number of secondary structures at Versailles. Among the most famous are the Orangerie—which was justly said to be "worthy of the Roman emperors" (above and below left), built between 1681 and 1686—and the Colonnade (below right), a great circle of paired columns.

The grove of the Baths of Apollo (below left), a famous work of Hubert Robert dating from 1778–1780, is one of the best-known features of the park. Little summerhouses (right), pavilions (below right), and statues of mythological characters (left) carved by the royal artists also decorate the landscape in every direction.

The Hall of Mirrors (preceding page), converted by Mansart from the loggia that connected the two central wings of the chateau, takes its name from the huge mirrors which stand opposite each window. The Hall of Mirrors links the various rooms of the royal apartments. It was also used as an audience chamber in which the king received ambassadors. Adorned with frescoes that celebrate the greatest victories of French arms, the Hall of Mirrors was the scene of the proclamation of the German empire following the defeat of France in the Franco–Prussian War.

Left and below, two views of the Hall of Peace, situated at one end of the Hall of Mirrors. It gets its name from the great painting by Le Moyne, which represents Louis XV giving peace to Europe. On the facing page is the Hall of War (below), the symmetrical twin of the Hall of Peace. It is dominated by the large medallion by Coysevox which shows Louis XIV on horseback. Above, a small drawing room and a bedroom, more modest in scale, yet full of pomp and luxury.

Above, the Salle de l'Oeil-de-Boeuf, named after the great oval or bull's-eye window which dominates it. An anteroom to the Great Hall, it owes its fame to a collection of stories and court gossip—all of it apocryphal—which gained a certain notoriety as "The Bull's-Eye Chronicles." The salon was the meeting place for those courtiers who had right of entrée, that is, ceremonial access to the king's bedchamber. Below left, a royal bedchamber, decorated entirely with fleurs-de-lis. Facing page, the fine desk made by Riesner for Louis XV, which stands in the middle of the king's cabinet intérieur. Above and below, the court Opera House, Gabriel's masterpiece, built entirely of wood for acoustical reasons.

The Chapel Royale, designed by Mansart, was built between 1699 and 1710. The chapel exalts the monarchy as much as the Deity, making it quite plain that kings acquire their power solely and directly from God, in accordance with the doctrine known as the divine right of kings. Mansart's plan distantly echoes, at least in theory, that of the Chapel of Charlemagne at Aix-la-Chapelle. Charlemagne appears as a saint in the frescoes on the vault. Even the chapel suffered from the inescapable drafts at Versailles. In Louis XV's reign, the members of the royal family had a kind of sentry box built over their seats so they could attend the services without perishing from cold.

Left, two views of the Méridienne, the small room decorated in 1781 by Richard Miqué for Marie Antoinette. The great stuffed couch in the center is its chief feature.

Above, the Salle du Pendule, with the great pendulum clock installed by Louis XV in 1754. The masterpiece of the engineer Passemant and the clockmaker Dautreau, it was later mounted in bronze by Caffieri.

Below right, the dauphin's library, with delicate polychrome decoration typical of the period from 1730 to 1760. The dressing room of Louis XV is at far right.

Following page, the palace seen across one of the great basins.

Versailles, France

Shortly before midday on September 5, 1638, at the royal chateau of St. Germain-en-Laye, a son was born to the French king, Louis XIII, and his wife Anne of Austria. Because the royal couple's marriage had been childless for twenty-three years, the birth of an heir to the throne was heralded throughout France. In Paris, peasants and nobility alike honored the newborn dauphin with military salutes, High Masses, bonfires, fireworks, and dancing in the streets. The infant, Louis le Dieudonné (Louis the God-given), insured the continuation of the Bourbon line on the throne of France.

The response to the birth of the dauphin was so joyful it would have been hard to predict that eleven years later, as King Louis XIV, he would be forced to flee Paris in the dead of night. He was able to re-enter only after a siege against his own subjects carried out by mercenary troops. When Louis XIV finally returned to Paris, he bore a profound distrust of the power of the masses. His suspicions of the lower classes and the petty machinations of Parisian political life eventually led him to choose an obscure village called Versailles, not far from the capital, as his retreat and his monument.

Le Métier du Roi

The recurrent political upheavals that took place during Louis' youth strengthened his conviction that the sovereign must have absolute power, which was summed up in the credo attributed to him: "L'état, c'est moi" (I am the State). He believed that the king's authority must be limitless and indivisible. The king must be consulted on every issue, decide every question, and sign every paper. Since the nobles had contributed to the decentralization of the monarchy, Louis decided to weaken their power. He also concluded that Paris was a threat to his rule and that its crowded web of streets denied him the space he needed to create a setting suitable for his new absolute monarchy. As one of the first major steps in his long reign as the Sun King, Louis XIV decided to centralize his authority—away from the civil disorders of Paris.

Establishing the royal seat away from Paris was not a new idea. In fact, Mazarin, the prime minister who succeeded Richelieu, had advised moving to Vincennes, where there was already a strongly fortified castle. But the Sun King did not approve of retreating to a castle hidden behind massive walls. Rather, he envisioned a palace at Versailles in the midst of a vast

The chateau of Versailles, seen from the park, as it appeared before Mansart's alterations and additions.

park where the king could create a grandiose setting in which to exercise his absolute monarchy, his "calling of kingship." Louis planned to control all of France through a new bureaucracy of officials at Versailles who would answer directly to him, bypassing the inefficient court network in Paris. Versailles would be both the instrument of his power and a monument worthy of his glory.

The men chosen to design the palace and its gardens were protégés of Fouquet, the superintendent of finances. This ambitious official, whose motto was *quo non ascendam?* (where will I not ascend?), had a chateau at Vaux-le-Vicomte that was the newest but also the most splendid of all French private residences. The reception he gave in 1661 for the king, the queen, and the court headed by the king's official mistress Louise de La Vallière, was worthy of a sovereign prince. The sumptuous meal was prepared by the chef Vatel, the ballet was composed by Molière (another of Fouquet's "discoveries") with scenery designed by the painter and decorator Le Brun and music by the composer Lully. And of course, there were fireworks in the park and lavish gifts for the guests. Three weeks later, however, Fouquet was arrested and imprisoned—the price he paid for attempting to live more regally than the sovereign.

The talents Fouquet discovered—the architect Le Vau, the landscape artist Le Nôtre, as well as Le Brun, Lully, and many others—were later recruited by the jealous king, who called upon them to transform Versailles into a proper setting for the Sun King's court.

The Court of Apollo

The transformation was dramatic. The hunting lodge Louis XIII had used at Versailles was a small building of dressed stone and brick. Constructed around three sides of a courtyard, it was set carelessly into the landscape. To build the new chateau, Le Vau surrounded the original building on three sides with a much larger U-shaped building. The open side was then arranged into two courtyards: the large outer Cour Royale, located between the two wings, and the inner Cour de Marbre, surrounded by the original building. The king's splendid bedchamber, at the center of the chateau, was the symbolic and architectural focus of the entire building. Joining the two arms of the U was an arcaded loggia which faced the park. Three grand carriage ways converged on the forecourt of the chateau. Below the chateau, Le Vau built a series of parterres or formal gardens that led to five avenues which stretched out radially, seemingly toward infinity.

The scale of Versailles is majestic. The parterres, for example, embellished with elaborate patterns formed by configurations of flowers and trees, occupy more than a third of a square mile. The distance from the loggia of the chateau to the Basin of Apollo at the end of the garden is nearly

Facing page, a plan of the Grand Trianon, where the king retreated to an environment less formal and exhausting than that of the great palace.

Below, Louis XIV, the Sun King, who made Versailles the capital of his kingdom.

Right, two seventeenth-century views of the chateau from the avenues that approach it. The mansard roofs are missing from the first illustration. Added later, they appear in the second picture.

two-thirds of a mile. The main access roads, constructed at a time when they were used primarily by pedestrians and a few carriages, are from 225 feet to 240 feet wide.

Between 1668 and 1671, the size of this impressive park was more than doubled. Le Nôtre's design called for a cruciform Grand Canal (one mile long by more than two-thirds of a mile wide) to replace the central avenue below the parterres. At the end of the canal, a new series of ten ave-nues stretched out. The parterres were re-designed, and many of the flower beds were replaced by pools and fountains.

These innumerable fountains are still the wonder of Versailles. During Louis' reign, they were the gathering place for royal functions. Foreign ambassadors presenting their credentials to the court were favored with a tour of the fountains. Louis considered the fountains to be of such importance that he went to the trou-ble of setting down instructions, in pains-taking detail, for their proper use. An ex-cerpt from his literary efforts written in 1672 sheds some light on his personal stake in the Versailles fountains:

It is the King's wish that the fountains always work in the following order when he arrives at Versailles; and when he wishes otherwise, he will send word. When His Majesty arrives by the pond road, the master fountaineer will be careful to turn on the water: in the Pyr-

Above, the palace after the extensive work carried out by Mansart, in what is almost its final form. Not only did Mansart add the two great wings set back on either side, but he also enclosed the loggia in the center of the building overlooking the park, creating the Hall of Mirrors.

amid, in the Allée d'Eau, in the Dragon, and he will take careful measures to insure that these fountains reach their perfection at the moment that His Majesty is looking at them from the other end of the road. Whatever side His Majesty arrives from, he wishes that the fountains of the Courtyard and the Siren are working when he arrives.

As the fountain of the Pavilion cannot function unless the Pyramid is stopped, the under-fountaineer in charge of these two fountains must make certain that he does not stop the Pyramid before His Majesty has entered the little avenue of the Pavilion and cannot see the Pyramid. Then he must at once switch the water to the Pavilion before His Majesty comes within sight of it.

At first, most of the water for the fountains was pumped from the marshy area around Versailles. When this source no longer yielded enough water, a gigantic and cumbersome machine was built nearby at Marly, raising the water of the Seine to the top of a hill 525 feet high so that it could flow down into the royal gardens.

The creation of the park at Versailles marked the beginning of the tradition of large-scale, planned gardens in France. A contemporary map or plan of Versailles would reveal the extent of the carefully designed park, of which the huge palace seemed only a small detail. After a tour of Italy, the landscape architect Le Nôtre contemptuously remarked, "The Italians do not have gardens which approach ours, and they are absolutely ignorant of the art of making them." Styled after Le Nôtre's park at Versailles, lavish French gardens—crowded with pools and fountains—dominated the fashion of landscape architecture for a century, just as French political and intellectual thought dominated European society.

Le Nôtre reached the pinnacle of his fame with the park at Versailles. At a time when 500 livres was considered a good annual salary, Le Nôtre was earning 30,000. His studio could barely keep up with orders to design gardens for the nobility of France as well as for other sovereigns of Europe. However, it has been said that when Louis wanted to elevate the distinguished landscape architect to a position of nobility, Le Nôtre replied that he would like his coat of arms to picture three slugs on a cabbage leaf—a humble, perhaps specious, request.

The Royal Residence at Versailles

In comparison to the gardens, the chateau seemed rather small, even though it had been enlarged by Le Vau. Decorated with magnificent paintings by Le Brun, Coypel, Blanchard, Houasse, La Fosse, and Jouvenet, it housed precious objects of gold and silver made by the furniture workshops of Les Gobelins.

Nonetheless, the chateau accommodated the needs of the Sun King until 1677, when he decided to transfer the entire court and all government offices to Versailles. Suddenly, room had to be found for the royal family, the nobles, and the officials of the expanding bureaucracy. At Le Nôtre's suggestion, Louis chose the architect Jules Hardouin Mansart, grandnephew of François Mansart who invented a steeply pitched roof with jutting windows, still called the "mansard roof." Jules Mansart's ability was first tested by a commission to build a country house at Clagny for the king's mistress, Madame de Montespan. A demanding woman, she had already ordered that one house, built for her by Louis, be torn down since she scornfully considered it to be "worthy of a chorus girl." Mansart's success in this delicate and difficult task laid the foundation of his career and assured him the king's sympathetic ear.

Mansart directed work at Versailles from 1678 to 1708. His renovations gave the palace its final form and made it a model of grandeur imitated by other rulers wielding absolute power. It served as the prototype for other royal castles such as Schönbrunn, Caserta, Charlottenburg, and Peterhof.

Mansart had to make some colossal changes in order to enlarge the existing chateau. He enclosed the loggia, transforming it into the 230-foot-long Hall of Mirrors, which now joined the north and south wings of the palace via the halls of War and Peace. Each window facing the park was matched by a huge mirror, manufactured by Louis' royal factories. Like the halls of War and Peace, the Hall of Mirrors was decorated with frescoes by Le Brun representing outstanding events in the reign of the Sun King. The Hall of Mirrors also served as an access route to the royal apartments which Mansart built within the original palace structure.

Mansart also constructed a dazzling series of courtyards. He first redesigned the old façade at the Cour de Marbre. In front of the Cour Royale, he created an immense courtyard called the Cour des Ministres. The new courtyard was flanked by two huge blocks of buildings which stood farther apart than any buildings in Le Vau's original plan. The three access avenues in front of the Cour des Ministres met to form a parade ground, lined by two blocks of stables to the north and south. Mansart designed the series of courtyards to create the appearance of ever-increasing space. The distant façade of the chateau was framed by the three U-shaped structures on a slight slope, each opening out from the other. Perhaps Mansart's grandest vision was the king's apartment, which was at the precise center of this theatrical frame. Dominant, yet detached, the royal apartment was at the symbolic center of France and, by extension, at the center of the universe.

Additional structural changes were required to make the palace a suitable site for the government. At right angles to the wings of the original chateau, Mansart added two large blocks of buildings with internal courtyards to house the members of the king's court. This massive enlargement re-established the proper proportion between the chateau and the park. In addition, Le Nôtre's park benefited from Mansart's renovations. On the south side of the park, he created the elegant Orangerie, framed by the grand stairway of Cent Marches (100 Steps). The famous Colonnade in the garden was formed by a large and elegant circle of paired columns.

Certainly the best example of Jules Mansart's genius is the Chapel Royale, which was built between 1697–1710 at the junction between the new south wing and Le Vau's old palace. Dedicated to St. Louis, it has the form of a palatinate chapel with a royal tribune on the upper level overlooking the nave, which was reserved for the public. An arcade encircling the central nave supports the elegant Corinthian colonnade above. The acoustics are

The green summerhouse, with trees cut into architectural shapes, created by Le Nôtre in the park at Versailles.

excellent. Before the dedication, Louis XIV is said to have paid a visit to inspect the chapel and ordered that a motet be sung to test its acoustical qualities, which he approved.

The young architect's talents did not go unrewarded. In the highly rigid social structure of seventeenth-century France, this self-made man was elevated to a position of nobility. He gained great renown and wealth—earning the enormous sum of 60,000 livres a year and owning several chateaux and wide expanses of land.

The Setting of the Sun

By the end of the seventeenth century, Louis XIV's palace at Versailles was nearly complete. Versailles had burgeoned in the "time of daring," that period of the Sun King's reign between the death of Mazarin in 1661, which left Louis in sole control of the government, and 1679, when he began to suffer defeats in his foreign adventures. During those years, Europe had been dominated by the 200,000 men of the new French army. But the closing years of the century witnessed the dénouement of Louis' reign. The period of splendor and grandeur was over. Madame de Maintenon, the king's mistress whom he had secretly married, did not like the overbearing pageantry of glory, and she complained that in the name of grandeur she would be forced to "die symmetrically."

Louis came to share her feelings, oppressed by the enormity of what he had brought into being. Between 1679 and 1686, Mansart built a separate residence for the royal family at Marly. From 1687 to 1688, Mansart erected the Grand Trianon to be used as a country residence replacing the small pavilion Le Vau had constructed at the foot of the Grand Canal. Louis spent increasing amounts of time at the Grand Trianon, and he lived there exclusively from 1703 until his death, only going to Versailles for official ceremonies. He frequently explained that he had built Versailles for the court, Marly for his friends, and the Grand Trianon for himself.

Après Moi le Déluge

On September 1, 1715, four days before his seventy-seventh birthday, Louis died. In keeping with his respect for maintaining the dignity of the royal office, the dying king advised his five-year-old successor to "lighten the burden of your people, and do what I have had the misfortune not to do." He left a powerful bureaucratic France, but it was a state dependent on the ability of its sovereign to exercise his *métier du roi* at every turn.

He also left an immense and extravagant palace. Over the course of fifty years, the construction had cost over 100 million livres. As many as 35,000 people had worked on the palace at a time, and hundreds of artisans helped create the works of art, precious mirrors, and furnishings. Despite the grandeur of the surroundings, Voltaire described Versailles as an enormous inn filled with discomfort and human misery. The absence of sanitary facilities at the palace made life for the

Above left, Louis XV with his mistress, Madame de Pompadour, a woman of middle-class origin who was the only royal mistress to die in office.

Left, the Grand Trianon seen from its parterres. After it became the royal residence, the great palace came to be used only for official ceremonies and court rituals.

One of the greatest attractions of Versailles is its fountains. Above left, the fountain of Latona and underneath it a detail of the central figure. Above right, a cupid shooting an arrow of water.

court members uncomfortable. Yet whatever miseries may have existed, they could not completely overshadow the aura of splendor. All of Europe regarded Versailles as the epitome of taste and fashion.

Versailles survived a few additional alterations following the death of Louis XIV. The reign of Louis XV was a golden age for writers, poets, artists, and artisans. For his mistress, Madame de Pompadour, Louis XV built the Petit Trianon. A residence of clean, classical lines built by the royal architect Gabriel in 1752, the Petit Trianon exerted a major influence on American federal architecture.

A final age of splendor at Versailles occurred during the marriage of the ill-fated Marie Antoinette and King Louis XVI. For this royal couple, Gabriel added the Opera House to the north wing of the palace, then built a new wing and reconstructed one of the buildings on the Cour des Ministres. Gabriel's work represented the greatest change in the general plan of the palace since the era of Mansart's vast renovations. Marie Antoinette was responsible for commissioning the artificial rustic village known as the Hameau, built in the park of the Petit Trianon. The bucolic setting was designed to provide an area where the queen and her courtiers could play at being shepherds.

On May 5, 1789, their pastoral diversions were interrupted by the parliamentary États Généraux, its first meeting in 175 years. On June 20, the representatives of the Third Estate vowed in the famous Tennis Court Oath that they would not adjourn until they had written a constitution for France. On July 14, the Bastille fell. On October 6, an enraged mob marched from Paris to Versailles, forcing its way into the chambers of the king and queen. After 150 years, the struggle between the palace of Louis XIV and the city ended in victory for the city.

Sacked and abandoned, the palace at Versailles seemed destined to disintegrate along with the regime which had created it. Napoleon later restored the Grand Trianon, which he used as his favorite country home. (It was later used as a retreat for President Charles de Gaulle.) But when Napoleon was asked to restore the Sun King's palace, he replied, "I dare not." It was later restored by King Louis Philippe, the ruler who adopted the revolutionary tricolor and who, according to

VI.ᵐᵉ Cahier de ... *Costume François*

Lamartine, had so little sense of grandeur that the country rebelled against him out of sheer boredom.

In the last half of the nineteenth century, Versailles served as the backdrop for some of the most tragic events in the history of France. On September 1, 1870—the 155th anniversary of the death of Louis XIV—Napoleon III surrendered to the Prussian army. Revolution broke out in Paris, and the Prussians continued to advance. On January 18, 1871, King Wilhelm of Prussia was proclaimed kaiser of Germany in the Hall of Mirrors at Versailles, surrounded by Le Brun's paintings of the great victories of France. Later that same year, during the time of the Commune, the Hall of Mirrors was occupied by the republican deputies, who organized the "Army of Versailles"—a brutal, armed mob that marched to conquer Paris, taking no prisoners, thus completing the long history of antagonism that had existed between the palace and the city. A last ironic event took place at the close of World War I when the German delegation signed the Treaty of Versailles, attesting to the humiliation of their country in the same setting where Germany had humiliated France in 1871.

Versailles has been a national museum since the 1870s. Instead of royal carriages, air-conditioned buses filled with tourists now park in front of Mansart's stables. With the help of the most creative minds of his time, the Sun King brought fame and glory to Versailles, once an insignificant village. It remains today a supreme example of their genius.

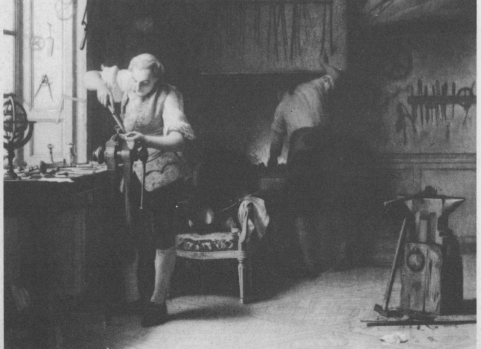

Above, Marie Antoinette of Austria, despised by the French and guillotined during the Revolution. A woman who loved frippery and luxury above all else, she had a husband with plain, middle-class tastes. Left, Louis XVI, who was more at home as a blacksmith than as a king.

The Forbidden City,

People's Republic of China

Preceding page, the Meridian Gate (Wumen). The bow-shaped River of Golden Water, frozen in its marble channel, curves through the Outer Court of the Forbidden City. The Meridian Gate is the southernmost, and largest, of the entrances into the city. In imperial times, only the emperor could pass through the center portal.

To the Chinese, the word for gateway (men) has a more complex meaning than mere opening. Decorative elements—brightly hued lacquers, glazed tiles, and delicately fashioned marble—endow each gateway with a symbolic significance. Visitors at right pass through an arch on the processional way through the Temple of Heaven complex in the Outer City.

Centuries of architectural and philosophical traditions have contributed to the evolution of the Forbidden City as a resonant world where forms, sizes, decorations, colors, numbers, directions, and elevations all implied something about the order of the universe. The five marble bridges that crossed the River of Golden Water (top left) corresponded to the Five Virtues of Taoist philosophy. An emperor, carried aloft on his palanquin, would cross the center bridge as he proceeded along the prescribed north–south axis on his symbolic journey through the city. He would pass between the two bronze lions (left and above)—representing imperial power—and be carried upward over the marble ceremonial ramp called the Dragon Pavement (center left, middle stair)

on his way to the Gate of Supreme Harmony (above). This passage was only a prelude to the greater height of the Hall of Supreme Harmony, where the enthroned emperor held court.

Far right, a sundial which symbolized the emperor's God-given ability to administer justice.

Right, a gilded dragon to ward off evil spirits.

The Purple Forbidden City (Tzu Chin Ch'eng), as it is sometimes called, does not take its name from the many red walls and buildings. Tzu, which means "purple," was really meant to suggest the polestar, implying the city's, and the emperor's, central position in both the temporal and spiritual spheres. Nevertheless, the time-worn red paint of the Eastern Flowery Gate (above left) appears purple. Appropriately, the imperial red of the past has been joined by the scarlet banners of the People's Republic of China. Today, the beautiful buildings of an imperial past—once so inaccessible—are open for the enjoyment of all, including the Chinese children gathering at right for a firsthand understanding of their heritage.

The roofs of imperial Peking are tiled in decorative colors that had specific symbolic meanings. The blue-tiled roof of the Temple of Heaven (above) spirals toward the firmament, while the green Temple of Earth (below left) is covered with bright yellow, suggesting fruits of the land. The Building of Felicitous Skies (below right) and the Tower of the Thousand Buddhas (below, far right) are roofed with the golden tiles that signify the Imperial City.

Following page, a misty snow accentuates the rhythmical curves of an imperial roof.

The Forbidden City, People's Republic of China

House of Sweet Melodies, Listen to the Swan, Hall of Supreme Harmony, Pure Mind Chamber, Hall of Celestial Purity—such buildings, found in Peking's Forbidden City, housed Chinese emperors and their courts for centuries. The elegant and poetic names still speak of mystery and fascination, but the city—once forbidden to all but the imperial court—is now open to everyone. Today, the many buildings enclosed within the walls of the Forbidden City—now the Old Palace—serve as a museum of a rich imperial past.

Yung-lo (Eternal Happiness), who began his reign in 1403, was the emperor responsible for initiating the construction of the Forbidden City and establishing Peking as a permanent Chinese capital.

However, Yung-lo by no means "discovered" Peking. Since the tenth century, Tartar invaders from the north had made a headquarters there; and by the late twelfth century, they had constructed imperial palaces on the site of what was to become the Forbidden City.

When Kublai Khan, the great Tartar leader of the Yüan dynasty, moved the seat of his government in 1264 to Chung-tu—later known as Peking—the city was transformed into a bustling center of trade and commerce and a cosmopolitan hub of many races and cultures. The Venetian adventurer, Marco Polo, was fascinated by the exotic richness and complexity of China and remained in Kublai Khan's court for nearly twenty years.

Upon moving his capital to the site of Peking, Kublai Khan named it Ta-tu, or "great capital." And he began to construct an enclosed city that became known as the Great Interior—a precursor of Yung-lo's Forbidden City.

Yung-lo was the fourth son of Hung-wu, the founder of the Ming dynasty who led a popular revolt against the foreign Tartars in 1368 and utterly demolished the magnificent court that Kublai Khan had established at Ta-tu. After conquering the city, Hung-wu decided not to make his capital there—a cold place, too near the northern enemies, and too difficult to defend—and moved his government back to the traditional Chinese capital of Nanking, or "southern capital."

Being the fourth son, Yung-lo had a poor chance of succeeding his father Hung-wu as emperor. The young lad tried to eliminate the problem by murdering his eldest brother. This method failed, however, and his father sent him packing to

Far left, Kublai Khan in 1200, who made his capital at Ta-tu. Yung–lo (center) renamed it Peking in 1421 and built the Forbidden City within its boundaries.

Below, an Italian map based on Marco Polo's descriptions of China.

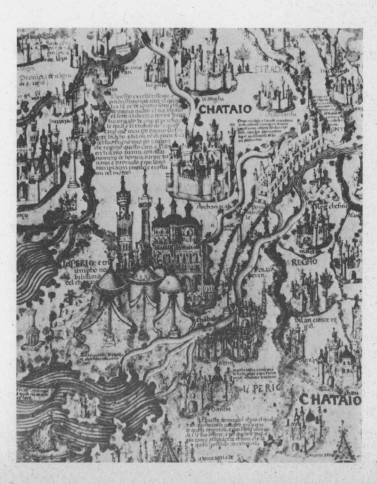

Left, the Forbidden City, where "earth and sky meet," in a sixteenth-century painting. To the Chinese, the city's alignment along the four compass points was essential in establishing its connection with the heavens.

Right, a Dutch delegation is received by the imperial guard (1671).

as to protect the ceremonial complexes.

The outermost of Peking's concentric rectangles, which housed lower ranking civil servants, was called the Inner City, but in the seventeenth century, it also became known as the Tartar City when the Chinese were chased out by the Tartars. Within its walls was the Imperial City, restricted for the use of high officials. At its center, reserved for the emperor, his family, and court attendants—most of whom by tradition were eunuchs—was the Forbidden City. This compound, about a thousand yards long from north to south and nearly eight hundred yards wide from east to west, lay heavily guarded and hidden behind high walls and a moat.

From Dream to Reality

Legend has it that the structure of the Forbidden City had been conceived by Yung-lo's tutor, a visionary monk, who one moonless night dreamed of a wonderful extraterrestrial city: the residence of the Lord of Heaven. The tutor suggested that the emperor's grand capital be designed as an emblem of the city that appeared in his dream. He reasoned that if the Heavenly Lord resided in the Purple Enclosure, a constellation formed by fifteen heavenly bodies turning around the polestar, then his son, the emperor, should live in a purple city at the center of the temporal world.

Yung-lo's residence became known as Tzu Chin Ch'eng, meaning "the purple city (ch'eng) of the polestar (tzu) where one cannot enter (chin)." Since the literal meaning of China (Chung-hua) is "the

Peking. In time, Yung-lo's exile led to an appointment as military governor, and he won the support of the armies of northern China. When his father died, Yung-lo had little trouble in marching to Nanking to secure the throne.

Realizing his base of power was in the north, Yung-lo decided to move his capital to Ta-tu. In 1404, he began to reconstruct the former Tartar capital which he renamed Peking, or "northern capital." Between 1404 and 1420, the new emperor

employed about 200,000 workers to begin building the imperial city, using wood from the forests of Yunnan and Szechwan. The new capital was constructed on the approximate site of Kublai Khan's Great Interior.

Yung-lo's Peking consisted of three roughly concentric walled areas, each an approximate rectangular shape. To the south, there also developed a fourth area, now known as the Outer City, which was later enclosed for strategic reasons as well

high incidence of suicide among this population was attributed to the chilling influence of the north wind.

Great importance was placed on building and landscape design based on patterns of squares and rectangles. Courtyards suggested the vastness of nature and balanced the geometric arrangement of the buildings, while asymmetric gardens contributed to a contrasting sense of natural release.

country at the center," it was logical to conceive of the Forbidden City as being at the center of the world. By establishing himself as the Son of Heaven, the emperor linked himself and his city to the divine forces in the universe.

The actual Forbidden City turned out to be as glorious as the dream that had inspired it. The palace was built, for the most part, in accordance with rules of spatial design first used during the Han dynasty in constructing the city of Chang-an

Below, a 1681 engraving of the observatory in Peking. Chinese astronomers, using a wide variety of instruments, had been practicing their art here for centuries.

Below right, travelers pass through one of the city's gates, which closed at sunset.

between 206 B.C. and A.D. 220. These ancient rules specified, among other things, that the principal buildings had to be aligned along a straight axis from north to south, flanked by a symmetrical arrangement of minor buildings on parallel axes. (This architectural convention fit well with Yung-lo's claim that his city had symbolic importance, because a centralized configuration of buildings would also serve as an emblem of the ordered heavens.) North was thought of as an evil direction. Since all invasions of China have originated in the north, it came to represent cold, dark, malevolent foreign elements. The only pavilions facing north belonged to the emperor's rejected concubines, and the

The Three Great Halls

The principal buildings of the Forbidden City lie along the north–south axis. The southernmost entrance to the city is the Meridian Gate (Wumen), the largest of the four gateways. Bells were struck softly as the emperor passed through the center portal and emerged into the Outer Court.

Before reaching the three great halls of state, the Gate of Supreme Harmony (Taihomen) must be passed. Guarded by two bronze imperial lions, this interior gate is elevated on a large terrace, which is reached by three marble staircases. Once through the gate, the three great halls are revealed consecutively along the north–south axis, elevated on an even higher—

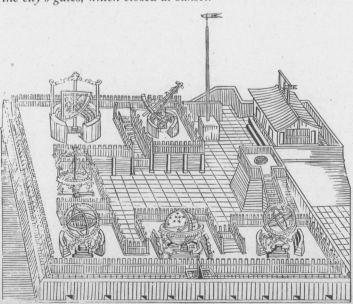

The authoritarian Dowager Empress Tz'u-hsi (above right) and the ineffectual emperor were forced to flee the Forbidden City in 1900 when international expeditionary troops (above) came to repress the Boxer Rebellion. Before leaving, the empress hid many valuable imperial treasures; she also had the emperor's Pearl Concubine thrown down a well because she wanted to accompany him. Twelve years later, China became a republic.

triple-tiered—terrace. These state buildings are the Hall of Supreme Harmony (Taihotien), the Hall of Middle Harmony (Chunghotien), and the Hall of Protecting Harmony (Paohotien).

The Hall of Supreme Harmony, the largest of all, contained the emperor's throne, raised high on a dais. Aside from state affairs, important ceremonies such as the Chinese New Year and the emperor's birthday were celebrated here. The enthroned emperor was surrounded by elaborately decorated vases, incense burners, screens, standards, sculptures of animals, and an orchestra of golden bells.

The emperor donned his majestic robes for his official appearances in the Hall of Middle Harmony, a 52-foot-square chamber. Here, once a year, he would also inspect the seeds for the new year's crop. In the Hall of Protecting Harmony—perhaps getting its name from the symbolic role it played in protecting the emperor from the evils of the north—state banquets were held. In this pavilion, the emperor also received scholars who had reached their highest level of attainment and were thus ready to enter government service.

The most intimate and hidden section of the Forbidden City was the series of three palaces—also aligned along the north–south axis—that comprised the personal apartments of the imperial family. These were the Palace of Celestial Purity, the emperor's bedchamber and secondary throne room, and the Palace of Vigorous Fertility, which was not where the emperor and empress united sexually but rather where the imperial seals were stored. Northernmost of the royal residences was the Palace of Earthly Tranquil-ity. In imperial China, this palace was the empress's private quarters, and it later became the royal bridal chamber. The entire room was decorated in the red color that was worn by the empress on her wedding night. "It was like the glow of a dying torch," wrote Pu-yi, who was the last Chinese emperor.

Osvald Sirén, who visited the Forbidden City in 1912, wrote that "the great number of buildings would make one's head spin were it not for the regularity of their arrangement and the uniformity of their style." A uniquely subtle awareness of rhythms and the calculated succession of planes and spaces is at the base of the equilibrium that governs the architecture of the Forbidden City. This equilibrium is also expressed intellectually in the web of myth, philosophy, and technology that made the city an elaborate symbolic world of self-proclaimed universal significance. Although no longer used as the imperial palace, the government maintains the Forbidden City as a museum, preserving the legacy of Chinese artistry.

Persepolis,

Iran

Preceding page, the excavated ruins of Persepolis in southwest Iran. Foreground, remains of warehouses and stores. The immense Hall of the Hundred Columns in the center was a 225-foot-square throne room. In the background to the right are the remains of the apadana, the ceremonial audience hall of King Darius (522–486 B.C.), one of the most energetic and capable of the Achaemenid kings.

Left, the ruins of the palace of Darius, framed by the columns of the apadana.

Center, the limestone terrace that supported the ceremonial and administrative buildings at Persepolis.

Bottom left and below, the winged bull (lamassu) which guarded the palace from evil forces. This ornamental motif (facing page) was adopted by Achaemenid artists from the Assyrians, who looked upon these gentle-faced bulls as potent protectors.

Above, the elaborately ornamented flight of steps leading to the apadana of Darius. The bas-reliefs (detail left) depict the Persian imperial guard known as the Ten Thousand Immortals. Covered by rubble for 2,000 years, these bas-reliefs have been well preserved.

Above, the curious, toothed battlements which, according to some scholars, symbolized that the king was as strong as a castle on a mountain. The battlements also appear as decorative motifs on the balustrades and over the bas-reliefs.

Below, the imposing, seemingly unending lines of guards flanking the steps up to the apadana. What other kings have had such a monumental and faithful bodyguard? Their cylindrical headgear with tight pleats identifies them as Persians.

Nothing of the apadana (above) remains except the solid stone gates and a few of the pillars. The more perishable brick walls and cedar roofs have been lost to time.

The tall columns (left) of the apadana *still loom over bas-reliefs of high Median dignitaries arriving at the great feast of the Persian New Year. They can be recognized as Medes by the high, rounded crown of their headgear. The Medes and the Persians were the most powerful of the ethnic groups united by Cyrus the Great (559–536 B.C.).*

Above, abstract decoration of a surviving stone gateway at the apadana.

Left, a carving in low relief representing the struggle between the Persian king and a winged, scorpion-tailed creature that symbolized evil.

Below, a capital in the form of a bull.

These bas-reliefs suggest the cosmopolitan spirit that must have prevailed at Persepolis. Each spring, subjects brought precious gifts from their native lands to present to the king of kings (details, bottom left and right). An inventory of the races and products of the Middle East, the bas-reliefs at Persepolis are an ethnological document of great importance, showing minute differences in dress and ornament and, with some stylization, distinguishing the features of various races.

Following page, the columns of the apadana; the Persian and Median guards; and (center) a winged disk—the symbol of Ahura Mazda, the great god who protected the fortunes of the Achaemenids.

Persepolis, Iran

The greatest remaining testament to the glory of the Persian empire is found at the ruins of its ancient capital, Persepolis, not far from Shiraz in southwest Iran. Persepolis was built by the Persians between 522 and 465 B.C. at the same time that their enemies, the Greeks, were building their great temples. Just as Athens came to symbolize the splendor of the ancient Greeks, so did Persepolis commemorate the energy and magnificence of the Persians, who rose from a small tribe to command one of history's most extensive—and short-lived—empires.

The Rise of the Persian Empire

The Persian empire was born in 550 B.C. when Cyrus the Great began his eleven-year rampage, overthrowing governments throughout the Middle East. First he deposed Astyages, king of the Medes, and occupied the northern provinces of Babylonia, establishing the base of the Achaemenid empire. Next he took on the wealthy Croesus, king of Lydia. In very little time, he conquered the Iranian plateau, Syria, Palestine, and the north of Arabia.

The empire continued to expand when King Cambyses II, the son of Cyrus, conquered the Nile Valley and became a pharaoh. Within just thirty years of Cyrus's staggering victories, the immense empire reached from the Indus River to Libya and from the Danube all the way to the Oxus River on the Aral Sea. In 522 B.C., when Darius I assumed control, the empire was at its height.

As king of this victorious and powerful empire, Darius wanted his capital at Persepolis to exalt the mighty Persian rulers and honor their conquests. Darius and his son Xerxes built most of Persepolis between 522 and 465 B.C., and its magnificence eclipsed the other three capitals of the empire: Pasargadae, where Cyrus the Great had erected the first monuments to Achaemenid power; Susa near the Persian Gulf; and Ecbatana in the rugged mountains to the north.

Curiously, Persepolis was founded on an unlikely site in the remote plain of Marv Dasht. Perhaps the location was chosen for its one natural treasure—an abundant spring. Water was considered an ultimate luxury in that arid region, and it served an indispensable function in ceremonial rituals, which were performed annually at Persepolis. As the national shrine of the empire, Persepolis provided a worthy setting for sacred rites honoring both the empire and its Achaemenid chieftains.

Persepolis was built on a grand scale, and the execution of its bold, spatial concept was uniquely Persian. Royal receptions, assemblies of representatives from all twenty-three provinces, and religious festivals convened in spacious audience halls. Surrounding the imperial buildings were royal apartments, administrative offices, barracks, stables, an arsenal, and an underground treasure house, which was protected in a labyrinth of tunnels dug deep into the surrounding rock.

Below, an illustration of Persepolis by Gailabaud, one of the more accurate of the early prints, which emphasizes the 50-foot-high artificial terrace on which Persepolis was built.

Below left, Alexander the Great, who razed Persepolis around 330 B.C.

Center, a frequent motif at Persepolis: the struggle between the king and the powers of evil.

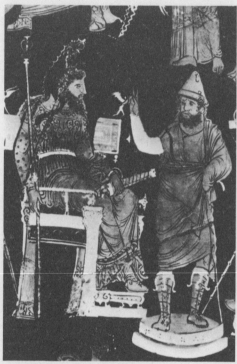

The complex rested on an immense limestone platform. Measuring almost 1,500 feet by 900 feet, the oblong terrace rose 50 feet above the valley plain. To build the platform, laborers removed almost ten million cubic feet of rock from Kuh-e Rahmat (Mount of Mercy). The dark gray stone was polished and hewed with precision, then bound in place with iron clamps.

Considering its size, Persepolis was remarkably unified. One of the original contributions of the Persians was a rigorously unified architectural concept—the use of the right angle as the supreme law of construction. Everything was governed by this principle, from the small rooms occupied by the palace servants to the great halls designed to exalt the Persian kings. In this way, the use of the right angle pervaded the architecture and contributed to a feeling of unity through repeated geometric forms.

The Egyptian principle of hypostyle construction (using rows of columns to support roofs and ceilings) was also a unifying influence. Square rooms had four, nine, sixteen, eighty-one, or one hundred columns, and rectangular rooms had six, ten, twenty, or more columns, depending on size. Typically, many of the massive, columned audience halls at Persepolis had entrance porticoes that created a pleasing transition between the open air of the courtyards and the interior of the monumental halls.

"... and its materials were brought from afar."

Cyrus's conquests of the Iranian plateau had brought the Persians into contact with countries rich in wood. The Persians frequently used wood, rather than stone, for their roofs. This practice allowed for greater distances between supports and for slender, elegant columns. The overall effect, typically Persian, imparted a feeling of fragility and spaciousness in the vast yet gracious halls and assemblies.

Darius I (522–486 B.C.), like Cyrus the Great before him, took full advantage of the diverse resources of his kingdom. Rather than tyrannizing his subject provinces, Darius respected their native traditions and skills, which he used to enrich his capital cities. The following lines from a stone inscription attributed to Darius relate how he went about consolidating his empire's wealth at Susa, a strategy he later followed at Persepolis, which he used as his spring palace:

I have built this palace, and its materials were brought from afar. The bricks were shaped and dried in the sun by the workmen of Babylon. The cedar wood trunks were brought from a mountain that is known as Lebanon. . . . The silver and ebony come from Egypt, and the wall decorations from Ionia.

The Great Hall

Darius, an energetic and effective administrator, enlisted laborers from the far reaches of his empire to build this little-used ceremonial city with its huge, colonnaded assembly hall—the *apadana*. Begun by Darius in 522 B.C. and completed by his two successors, Persepolis sums up the eclectic character of Persian architecture.

The cedar roof of Darius's 250-foot-square *apadana* rested on tapering columns which terminated in capitals composed of kneeling bulls placed back to back. The bull motif occurs frequently at Persepolis—and nowhere more spectacularly than in the gigantic-winged, Assyrian-inspired bulls guarding the gates of the entrance hall.

The *apadana* was buttressed by four corner towers, which housed service facilities and guard rooms. To approach the royal hall, it was necessary to pass through a monumental gateway—the Gate of All Nations—which must have reminded visiting dignitaries and foreign representa-

tives of the grandeur of the ceremonial capital.

The sacred, enclosed *apadana* was raised on a ten-foot stone terrace decorated with triple-tiered reliefs masterfully executed by the empire's most gifted artisans. Bas-reliefs also ornament the graceful, 22-foot-wide stairway which leads to the *apadana* from the northern façade. Some of the most famous reliefs at Persepolis depict a dignified procession of the Ten Thousand Immortals (the empire's

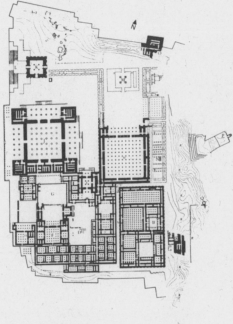

trusted bodyguards) who march past domestic scenes of peace and prosperity.

Other surviving reliefs, many of which have been protected by rubble through the centuries, commemorate the Procession of the Tributaries, a royal festival honoring the Persian king at the Norûz (Persian New Year). Originally painted in vivid colors, the reliefs show subjects—Lydians, Phrygians, Ionians, Egyptians, Arabs, and Ethiopians—laying gifts at the feet of the all-powerful Achaemenid em-

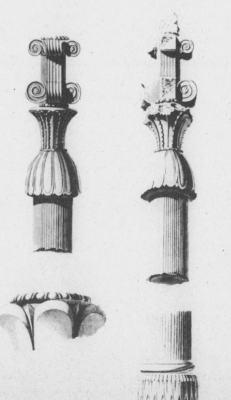

Left, the ground plan of Persepolis. The typically Persian composition consists of a dense, regular pattern of colonnaded squares and rectangles. To the left of center is the apadana. *The columns (below) are characteristically slender. Their voluted capitals once bore a system of wooden beams, many carved from the rare cedar of Lebanon. Other capitals bear the traditional double-bull motif. The Persian column is often fluted, with a molded base ornamented with floral motifs.*

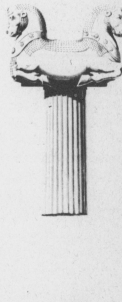

Right, a procession of male subjects offers tribute to the king. There was a taboo against representing women in royal art during this period.

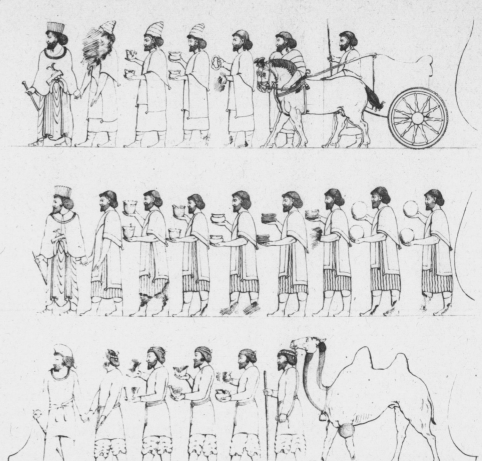

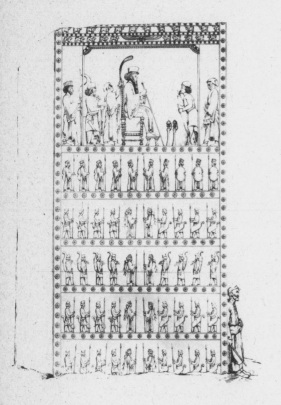

Above, the king of kings holding court, surrounded by his bodyguard.

peror. They also document the great variety of tributes brought from the twenty-three nations of the empire: vases and silks, jewels and silver coffers, and finely engraved weapons. Together, the bas-reliefs of the *apadana* and other ceremonial structures at Persepolis provide an observant record of local customs and foreign life-styles.

The great colonnaded rooms at Persepolis elucidate the differences between ancient Greek and Persian architecture of the fifth century. Greek architecture served a religious purpose which did not require large interior spaces. Persian architecture, in contrast, was political in nature, and the great halls at Persepolis were expressly designed to magnify the empire and the unifying power of the sovereign. Assembled at the massive assembly halls, subjects from each corner of the empire joined together to honor cooperation and peace among nations.

"King of the earth, far and wide"

Persepolis represented the heart of a vast, polyglot kingdom ruled by a sovereign king who was the earthly representative of the Persian god Ahura Mazda. An omnipotent ruler, the king of kings imposed a *Pax Persica* on the empire and enjoined his subjects to honor their solidarity at annual religious celebrations. The description of Darius the Great, preserved at Persepolis, is an eloquent testimony to his omnipotence and reveals the nature of the power once attributed to the Persian monarchs responsible for consolidating one of the world's most diverse kingdoms:

One king of many, one lord of many... the great king, king of kings, king of the countries possessing all kinds of peoples, king of the great earth, far and wide.

By the time Alexander the Great had risen to power, less than two hundred

years after Darius founded Persepolis, the Persian empire had weakened considerably. Abandoning its policy of maintaining peace, the empire attempted to crush a few small Greek city-states. Experienced warriors, the Greeks were able to defeat the Persians, despite the Persian advantage in numbers. The empire was felled forever when Alexander the Great burned down Persepolis to avenge the Persians' burning of the Acropolis in Athens. In one night, following four years of fighting, the capital and symbol of the powerful ancient empire was reduced to ashes. Since then, the spring whose water sustained Persepolis has gone dry, and the desert sun beats down on the few surviving remains of what was once the national shrine of the Persian empire.

Preceding page, the Kremlin in winter. Behind the brick wall is the Great Palace of the Kremlin. Also visible are the gilded pinnacles and onion domes of the old cathedrals built during the fourteenth century. Far right, the Spassky Tower. To its left is the Cathedral of Michael the Archangel, where members of the royal family were buried; and to its left is the great bell tower built for Ivan the Great. The small Cathedral of the Annunciation, which was the czar's private chapel, lies between the bell tower and the palace.

Above, the seventeenth-century pyramidal roofs of the Kremlin towers. In the background is the spectacular Cathedral of St. Basil in Red Square. Below right, the Spassky Tower, the most massive of the Kremlin's twenty towers. Below left, the exuberant stone decoration of the Spassky Tower. Facing page, one of the corner towers of the Kremlin. In the background is the bell tower of Ivan the Great.

Unlike many other former palaces, the Kremlin continues to play an active role in the nation's affairs. The expansive Palace of Congresses (above), built in the 1960s, is the most recent structure to be erected within the Kremlin walls. The old cathedrals of the czars can be seen in the background.

Below, a corner of the Kremlin, dominated by the huge bulk of the star-topped Spassky Tower and the Cathedral of St. Basil.

A variety of architectural styles can be found within the Kremlin walls. The Cathedral of Michael the Archangel (above) was the second church to be built at the Kremlin by Italian architects.

Right, the austere arsenal built for Peter the Great, nestled against the walls. The Trinity Tower, which resembles the Spassky Tower, is along the wall to the right.

Above, Lenin's tomb, a massive step-pyramid of red granite. Every day a seemingly endless line of people views Lenin's remains inside the tomb.

Right, the brightly colored Cathedral of St. Basil. The dramatic coloration of the decoration was added to the exterior long after the structure was completed.

Facing page, Red Square, the huge plaza adjacent to the Kremlin illuminated with a display commemorating the Russian Revolution. Since the sixteenth century, Red Square has been the heart of Moscow. On one side are the Kremlin walls and the Spassky Tower. In the distance is the fantastic Cathedral of St. Basil. Lenin's tomb (adjacent to the Kremlin wall) contains the embalmed corpse of the founder of the U.S.S.R.

Left, the Palace of the Senate, the only building added to the Kremlin by Catherine the Great. After abandoning an earlier plan of tearing down the Kremlin to build a gigantic, Versailles-like palace complex, her less ambitious legacy to the Kremlin took the form of this single example of eighteenth-century neoclassicism.

Left center, the Granovitaya Palace (Faceted Hall), the czar's official residence, built in the late fifteenth century by two Italian architects, Marco Ruffo and Pietro Solario. It is perhaps the most Italianate of those buildings at the Kremlin designed by Italian architects. Its façade is reminiscent of many northern Italian palaces. The palace is named after the stylized pattern of its rusticated ornamental masonry of the façade.

Below left, the Terem, which was the czar's private residence. Its exuberant decoration, excellent workmanship, and lively colors make it a fine example of seventeenth-century Russian architecture.

Facing page, two views of St. Basil's, a dramatic Russian response to the Renaissance classicism of some earlier Kremlin buildings, whose styles, like their architects, have been imported from the west. Unlike the more severe buildings of the Italian architects, St. Basil's incorporates lively features indigenous to Russian architecture: traditional ornamental motifs derived from wooden buildings, bright colors, and the division of large volumes into a series of minor ones. Here, in fact, a group of smaller churches is clustered around a central church. According to legend, Ivan the Terrible had the architects of St. Basil's blinded so that they could never again make anything so beautiful. The story is untrue but reflects the spirit of the era in which the cathedral was built.

ГРАЖДАНИНУ МИНИНУ И КНЯЗЮ ПОЖАРСКОМУ
БЛАГОДАРНАЯ РОССІЯ. ЛѢТА 1818

Above left and right and facing page, the bell tower of Ivan the Great. Ivan commissioned the building from the Italian architect Marco Bono in the early years of the sixteenth century to house a large number of bells. A century later, Boris Godunov completed the work as part of the celebration for his own coronation as czar by building the upper stories of the octagonal tower. Reaching a height of 260 feet, the tower is the tallest building in the entire Kremlin. It contains no fewer than thirty-three bells.

Left, the Cathedral of Michael the Archangel, designed in the early sixteenth century by Alvise Novi, who modeled the cathedral after the Cathedral of the Assumption at Vladimir. However, the ornamentation, such as the large, decorative shells filling the exterior arched pediments, is typical of the Italian Renaissance.

The bulging, gilded cupolas of Holy Moscow, long a symbol of the city, echo an ancient tradition of the wooden architecture in Russia.

Above, the small, finely crafted cupolas of the Cathedral of Our Savior Behind the Golden Grill, surmounted by Byzantine crosses.

Left, the cupola on top of the bell tower of Ivan the Great.

Right, a cluster of cupolas on the Cathedral of the Annunciation. This small church, the work of Russian architects, served as the chapel of the royal family for hundreds of years.

Since the Russian Revolution, the churches and palaces of the Kremlin have been converted into museums, displaying the wonderfully rich artistic and historic treasures of imperial Russia.

Facing page, the Cathedral of the Assumption. Used as a model for all subsequent Russian churches, it was built between 1475 and 1479 by the Italian architect Fioravanti. Although roughly based on the Cathedral of the Assumption at Vladimir, much of the ornamental detail is that of the Italian Renaissance.

Above, the canopied pew of Ivan the Terrible. Made of finely carved wood, it is a masterpiece of sixteenth-century craftsmanship and artistry.

Above right, the richly ornamented doorway of the Cathedral of the Assumption, decorated with icons.

Below right, a section of the iconostasis, the screen dividing the sanctuary from the congregation, in the Cathedral of Michael the Archangel.

Russian mosaics and frescoes, which were much influenced by Byzantine art, abound not only in the churches but also in the palaces of the Kremlin.

Above, the frescoes in the Golden Room of the Granovitaya Palace. Highlights of Russian history are painted on a gold background. The vaulted roof is supported by one immense central pillar.

Below, the czar's bedchamber, in an ornate restoration of the nineteenth century.

Right, the czarina's chamber in the private residence of the Terem. The frescoes depict scenes from the life of Christ.

The great tradition of Russian icons is well represented in the Kremlin.

Top, left to right: the twelfth-century icon of St. George Victorious; an angel from an icon of the Trinity; a detail from the icon of Peter and Paul (both fourteenth century).

Center, left to right: the Madonna; St. John; and St. John the Baptist—all details from a Greek icon.

Bottom, left to right: a fourteenth-century icon of "The Chastening Eye of the Lord" and the Madonna of Vladimir, the most venerated of the Russian icons.

Facing page, an icon of the Last Supper.

The Oruzheinaya Palata, the armory built by Constantin Thon for Czar Nicholas I in the middle of the nineteenth century, houses a collection of artistic and historic treasures from imperial Russia.

Above, the English parade carriage of Boris Godunov, a gift from Queen Elizabeth I.

Left, the golden throne encrusted with precious stones, given to Boris Godunov by the shah of Persia.

The Museum of Weapons, originally the arsenal of the Kremlin, gradually became the treasure house where precious gifts from foreign dignitaries were stored.

Above, the elaborate ceremonial trappings of the czar's horse.

Below, left to right: the diamond- and pearl-studded crown with an enormous ruby at the base of the cross made for the coronation of Peter the Great; the crown of Ivan V; the ceremonial orb, a globe divided into two hemispheres below a cross, symbolizing power.

Following page, the Cathedral of St. Basil (left) and the vast Spassky Tower (right) seen across the expanse of Red Square.

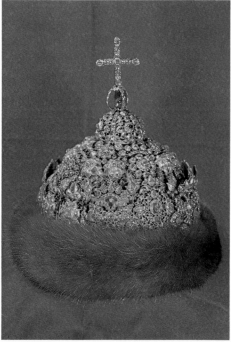

The Kremlin, U.S.S.R.

"In the evening we went incognito to the Kremlin, an old castle used as a residence by the Czars." In her memoirs, Sophie Friederike Auguste of Anhalt–Zerbst records her first visit to the Kremlin on the occasion of her engagement in June 1744. Later, she was rebaptized into the Russian Orthodox Church with the name of Catherine Alekseyevna (the name "Sophie" was taboo at the Russian court and had been since the days of Sophie Alekseyevna, Peter the Great's sister who had been perhaps overly fond of intrigue) and passed into history as Catherine the Great, empress of all the Russias.

Far more eloquent than Catherine—little more than fifteen at the time of the ceremony—was the Marquis de Custine, a Frenchman who came from the bourgeois Paris of the early nineteenth century and lived in Russia during the time of Nicholas I's Holy Alliance. His *Lettres de Russie* have been for the best part of 150 years the intellectual Baedeker for any Westerner who wants to understand the mystery of Russia. "Jail, palace, sanctuary, bastion against invaders, Bastille against the nation itself, the support of tyrants, the prison of the people." Thus the marquis, who combined a sharp critical sense with a succinct style, summed up his perceptions of the Kremlin of Moscow.

The Kremlin, a walled city occupying ninety acres in the heart of Moscow, has embodied the spirit of Russia for centuries. Besieged by the Golden Horde, scarred by fire, blown up by Napoleon, and damaged during the Bolshevik Revolution, the Kremlin has survived violence and assault—but not without almost continual alteration and restoration. The evolution of the Kremlin from a small wooden fortress to a Renaissance palace and, finally, to a modern administrative and political center often reads more like legend than history. It offers a revealing glimpse into the colorful, sometimes enigmatic, history of the Russian state.

Palace, Sanctuary, and Bastion Against Invaders

In the twelfth century, Russia was filled with hundreds of small fortifications called *kreml'* which surrounded feudal estates, churches, and marketplaces. Kremlins of major importance existed in the cities of Kiev, Novgorod, Vladimir, and Suzdal, but even peasant villages were protected by fortifications during times of special threat.

Although the Moscow area had been populated for some time, historians can only trace the origin of its development back to the year 1147. Historical annals record that in this year Prince Yuri Dol-

Above, Ivan III (Ivan the Great), who solidified the power of Moscow and initiated the expansion of the Kremlin.

Right, a stylized view of the Kremlin in 1556.

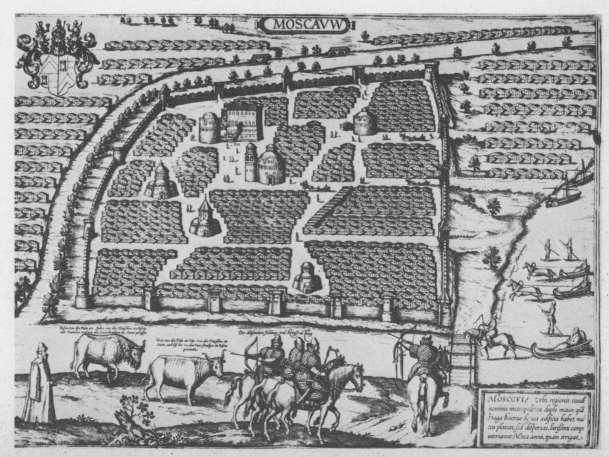

Left, Boris Godunov, a statesman who was the subject of a Pushkin play and a Moussorgsky opera.

Right, Ivan the Terrible, who first formally adopted the title "czar" (caesar) and under whose rule Russia truly became a centralized state.

The white stone walls (above) of the Kremlin, which replaced the earlier wooden fortifications, more than once helped stave off assaults of the Tartars.

goruky invited Prince Svyataslov of Novgorod–Seversky to attend a banquet in Moscow, where he had turned his country estate into a two-and-a-half-acre wooden fortress.

At the time, Moscow was a burgeoning village, using its strategic position at the junction of the Neglinnaya and Moscow rivers to develop its commerce. Moscow was on the water route serving the Byzantine–Scandinavian trade between the Caspian and Baltic seas, and its favorable location enabled it to benefit from the overland routes that ran from Smolensk to Vladimir and from Novgorod to Ryazan.

It was here that Moscow's first kremlin was built, consisting of a single wooden wall fortified with dirt ramparts and ditches. This kremlin, however, burned like matchsticks before the Mongol invasion in the thirteenth century. In a wave of destruction, the Golden Horde sacked and burned Moscow, Vladimir, Suzdal, and Kiev. But true to the Russian spirit, Mo-

scow emerged—phoenix-like—from the devastation and re-established itself as a vital settlement, where artisans and merchants could prosper. And by the end of the thirteenth century, Moscow had reconstructed its kremlin, which emerged as a formidable stronghold.

First Steps Toward Unification

Under the leadership of Daniel, prince of Moscow, the city continued to grow and came to inherit the political and religious strengths of Kiev, which had been the center of Russian culture in the eleventh century. (Daniel was the son of the heroic prince Alexander Nevsky, so called because he had successfully repelled Swedish invaders at the Neva River.) The destructive Tartar raids had subsided, yet their cultural and political influence remained so potent that, in 1327, one of Daniel's successors, Ivan Kalita, led an army against his compatriots who refused to pay the tribute exacted by the Tartars. Kalita (meaning "moneybags") soon used this influence and Moscow's expanding commercial strength to become grand prince of Moscow and tax collector for the

Tartars. He began a campaign to unify the villages into a cohesive Russian state, establishing Moscow as the center of an enlarged principality.

Another significant step toward increasing the strength of Moscow occurred when the leader of the Russian church, the metropolitan bishop, moved his seat there from Vladimir in 1326. To honor the bishop's decision, Ivan Kalita ordered a new stone church, the Cathedral of the Assumption, to be built. A wooden ducal palace and the Cathedral of Michael the Archangel followed, each surrounded by wooden walls that were destroyed by fire between 1331 and 1337. When they were reconstructed, Ivan's builders used thick oak instead of pine, hoping to make the walls more fireproof. None of these buildings have survived, but the original site, known as Cathedral Square, has remained the heart of the Kremlin.

When Ivan's grandson Dmitri came into control of Moscow, he turned the city against the Tartars. A stone fortress with turreted white walls was built between 1359 and 1374 to replace the wooden kremlin. In 1380, Dmitri defeated the great Mongol khan and his warriors on the banks of the Don River, and he became known as Dmitri Donskoi in honor of his victory. This marked the beginning of

Moscow's resistance to the legendary invincibility of the Golden Horde. Only two years later, Moscow was sacked and burned, but it was quickly rebuilt and once again grew to a position of strength and importance.

Not until the late fifteenth century, under the crafty and resourceful Ivan the Great, did the Tartar domination of Russia come to an end. Ivan refused to pay the tribute demanded by the Tartars, and it was said that he actually spat on the khan's coat of arms. Ivan's dominion was further strengthened by his annexation of the mercantile center of Novgorod, making Moscow the ruling city of a newly centralized Russian state.

In his rise to power, Ivan the Great began to call himself "czar," a Russian term derived from the Roman title "caesar," which means emperor. He had married a Byzantine princess, the niece of Constantine XI, who was the last emperor of the Eastern Roman Empire. Ivan further solidified the identification of the Eastern Roman Empire with Moscow by adopting the Byzantine insignia, the two-headed eagle, which continued to symbolize imperial Russia until the time of the Revolution in 1917.

The Crown of Power

Encouraged by his wife, who had been educated in Rome, Ivan sent an envoy, the boyar Simeon Tolbuzin, to Italy to recruit the best talent available to rebuild Moscow. Tolbuzin returned with Ridolfo

The czar (below) passes the Cathedral of St. Basil on the way to his citadel within the Kremlin walls.

MOSCVA

Above, a map of seventeenth-century Moscow, showing how the city grew from its original nucleus within the Kremlin.

Right, an unusual representation of the young Peter the Great being instructed by his tutor in the military arts.

Below, Catherine the Great, the autocratic ruler of Russia during the Enlightenment.

Fioravanti of Bologna, also known as Aristotle for his abilities as an architect and engineer as well as his expertise in military fortifications, hydraulics, and pyrotechnics. In order to carry out such an involved undertaking, Fioravanti found it necessary to set up a brickworks and to train workmen in contemporary technical building processes.

In four years, Fioravanti rebuilt the Cathedral of the Assumption within the walls of the Kremlin. Fioravanti's design combined local traditions with Italian architectural principles; the result was more Russian than Renaissance. The architect was also influenced by the rectangular plan and staggered cupolas of Byzantine churches. He redefined the interior space, building five apses rather than three. Based on the twelfth-century Byzantine Cathedral of the Assumption in Vladimir, Fioravanti's Cathedral of the Assumption was used as a model by architects throughout Russia. The walls were of white limestone with brick beneath the domes and vaulting. The height and spacious interior of the cathedral generated a sense of light and space. The cathedral was used for coronations and as the burial vault of the Muscovite metropolitans and patriarchs—the Russian Orthodox clergy.

The Russian architects of the adjacent Cathedral of the Annunciation, the court church of the Moscow princes, were influenced by Fioravanti when they built their smaller but more elaborate church between 1482 and 1490. Constructed on the foundations of the fourteenth-century church, the Cathedral of the Annunciation had a richly decorated interior; the floor was paved with mosaics of jasper and agate, and the walls were covered with frescoes. The success of these Russian architects and masons, trained first by Fioravanti, prepared the way for other Italian architects at the Kremlin.

In 1485, Fioravanti was followed by two Italians, Marco Ruffo and Pietro Solario, who built the Granovitaya Palace (Faceted Hall), similar to the later Palazzo dei Diamanti in Ferrara, Italy. The palace, the oldest public building in Moscow, was named after the faceted stone on its

Above, an engraving of Red Square—then Moscow's market square. Created by demolishing the houses that once clung to the outside of the walls, Red Square was also used as a parade ground and as the site of public executions.

façade. The ground floor consisted of administrative offices, and the second story was a large reception hall and throne room. Called the Golden Room, it was named after the frescoes depicting scenes from Russian history painted on a golden background. The vaulted ceiling was unusual in that it was supported by a single central pillar rather than the large number of columns usually needed to support a roof of comparable size. Since women were not allowed to attend the receptions of the czar, there was a room above the portal from which the czarina and princesses could observe the functions in the Golden Room.

Another Italian architect, Alvise Novi, built the Cathedral of Michael the Archangel between 1505 and 1509 on the site of the original fourteenth-century church. Of traditional Russian design with five domes, Novi's church incorporated more Italian motifs than any of the other churches in Cathedral Square. The façades were later divided into sections separated by pilasters (flat ornamental columns set onto the wall), and the interior walls were covered with murals and icons of the fifteenth, sixteenth, and seventeenth centuries. Even the pillars bore portraits of historical figures. The large gilded wooden iconostasis (the screen dividing the congregation from the sanctuary) was forty-two feet high. The cathedral's nave holds the remains of grand princes and czars from the time of Ivan Kalita to Peter the Great, except for Boris Godunov whose body was moved in 1606.

An enormous bell tower was designed to house Ivan's vast collection of bells, including the sixty-three ton Bell of the Assumption. The lower part of the tower was built between 1532 and 1543, and the belfry and cupola, added by Boris Godunov in 1600, completed the belfry honoring Ivan the Great.

Fortifying the Kremlin

The task of replacing Dmitri Donskoi's white stone walls of the Kremlin with red brick fortifications took two Italian architects and their workers ten years. The old walls were removed in small sections and replaced immediately with brick so that there were no gaps in the fortification of the palace. The Kremlin was enlarged to cover sixty acres. The walls alone were over a mile and a third long and included a succession of distinctive towers built over a period of two hundred years.

In the event of invasion, the enemy could be seen from the towers, and warning bells were rung to give people time to take refuge inside the Kremlin walls. Each of the Kremlin's twenty towers had a firing platform and a platform for archers. But the towers themselves were stylistically and functionally diverse. Some towers housed secret passages; others commemorated saints and exalted rulers. Studied together, the towers trace the evolution of defensive strategies at the Kremlin and reflect the whims of some of Russia's most colorful rulers.

Five of the towers were used as gates. The main gate was in the Spassky Tower, named for the finely worked icon of Christ over the gate. Solario built the tower, which had a drawbridge over the moat, in 1490. In 1625, Christopher Galloway, a Scottish architect, added an elaborate tower, a steeple, and a clock. The present clock was installed in 1851, and its chimes are broadcast daily over Radio Moscow. One of Lenin's first acts in 1918 was to change the tune they played from "God Save the Czar" to the "International."

The Nikolsky Tower, next to the Spassky Tower, is remarkable for its icon of St. Nicholas over the doorway. Built in 1491, the tower was blown up by Napoleon's troops in 1812 and rebuilt in 1820. In that same year, Napoleon also destroyed the Borovitsky Tower (Forest

Top, an old view from within the Kremlin walls.

In 1812, Napoleon captured Moscow (bottom), only to watch the city burn while he sat helpless within the Kremlin.

Tower), which was named after earlier wooden towers in Moscow. The upper half of the Borovitsky Tower had been added in the seventeenth century.

The Sobakina Tower and the Tainitsky Tower (Tower of Secrets) were not only useful for defense but also for clandestine operations. The Sobakina Tower contained a secret well and a hidden exit leading to the Neglinnaya River. The Tainitsky Tower, built by Antonio Friasine in 1470, provided secret passage to the Moscow River. It was partially demolished by Catherine the Great, and construction on a new tower was begun on the same site in 1771 and was completed two years later.

Friasine also built the Water-Hoist Tower, which brought water from the Moscow River through an aqueduct to the Kremlin palaces. Another interesting tower, the Blagoveschenski Tower (Tower of the Annunciation) was connected to the old Cathedral of the Annunciation. It was used as a prison during the reign of Ivan the Terrible, who liked to watch executions from a wooden arcade that became the site for the Czar's Tower built in 1680.

St. Basil's in Red Square

Under Ivan the Great, the Kremlin was transformed into a Renaissance palace, and the city was enlarged to accommodate the needs of the capital. His grandson, Ivan the Terrible, who ruled from 1533 to 1584, exercised his absolute power to forge all of Russia into a unified state that included the Baltic lands and Siberia. Calling himself "Czar of all the Russias," Ivan dissolved the Tartar kingdoms of Kazan and Astrakhan, and the lands along the Volga River became the property of his Russia. During this time, the exuberant spectacle of St. Basil's Cathedral was built in Red Square. Ivan the Great had demolished houses, taverns, and churches in order to create an immense space adjacent to the palace to be used as a parade ground. Called Red Square (the word *krasnyi* in Russia means both "beautiful" and "red"), the area was the site of public executions, royal decrees, markets, and the annual ceremonial presentation of the czar to the people.

St. Basil's was built to commemorate Moscow's victories over the Mongol invaders and Ivan's annexation of the Kazan and Astrakhan lands. The cathedral, built from 1555 to 1560, consists of nine churches, each dedicated to a particular saint on whose day a Muscovite victory took place. The legend that Ivan had blinded the Italian architect of St. Basil's so that he would never again create anything so beautiful is untrue, but it does offer a telling insight into Ivan's complex character. The cathedral was actually designed by two Russians, named Barma and Postnik, and presents a distinctly Russian response—joyous and triumphant—to the staid influence of classical

Italian architecture around it. The exterior of the cathedral is colorful and profusely decorated. The feeling of Russian traditional wooden architecture appears in the stonework. In the seventeenth century, the church was painted in subdued tones. In the eighteenth century, it was repainted in the striking colors that can be seen today. The bulbous domes on top of each of the towers are elaborately carved and brilliantly colored. The lively Cathedral of St. Basil and the massive Spassky Tower opposite it are two of the most dramatic sights of Red Square.

The Empty Cradle of the Romanovs

The period of growth and expansion of the Kremlin was at its peak under Ivan the Terrible. During the seventeenth century, the Romanov dynasty, descended from the wife of Ivan the Terrible, controlled

An old panoramic view (below) reveals the turreted walls and gilded cupolas of the Kremlin rising above a still rustic Moscow.

Russia. Although only a few additions were made to the Kremlin, in 1635, three Russian architects built the Terem (Attic Palace) which housed the royal family and was the center of life for the women. Based on the traditional style of architecture used in wooden dwellings in Russia, it resembled three peasant houses placed next to one another. The two-storied Terem contained an attic and observation tower. The portals were carved in high relief, and the windows were of colorful mica.

Pyramidal spires were also added to the towers surrounding the Kremlin. Heavy ornamentation was added to the Cathedral of the Annunciation, and the Steps of Ivan the Terrible were added in 1572. The three-storied Patriarch's Palace, built in a revival of the Vladimir–Suzdal style, was constructed in 1656 adjacent to the Church of the Twelve Apostles for the patriarch Nikon.

Boris Godunov's completion of the bell tower built by Ivan the Great was a source of dissatisfaction among the people. The gilded cupola of the bell tower was finished during a period of great famine when people were literally dying in the streets. Throughout the century, a succession of uprisings was generated by the growing antifeudal sentiments of peasants in Moscow.

When Peter the Great became czar in 1682, he began to strengthen the economic and cultural life of Moscow by building schools and factories and by starting the first Russian newspaper. Peter the Great's desire for greater technological advancement led him to realize that Russia's isolation from the rest of Europe was an impediment to Russian progress. Peter laid the foundations for a Russian "window on the West" by moving the capital from Moscow to a new city on the Neva River— St. Petersburg, now Leningrad. In an effort to establish the new capital as an enduring center, he did not allow any construction in stone outside of St. Petersburg. Pushkin described his transfer of political power in a famous statement:

And Moscow bowed to the new capital, as the Queen Dowager bows to the young queen.

In 1812, all of Moscow was rocked by Napoleon's siege. Most of the city was devastated by a fire lasting for three days. Parts of the Kremlin were blown up by the French. French cavalry horses occupied the Cathedral of the Assumption, one of the buildings to survive. Napoleon's troops used icons as firewood and looted the cathedrals of great quantities of gold

and silver. When the French abandoned the city, Moscow was in ruins.

But within a few years, the Kremlin walls were reconstructed, the Neglinnaya River was put into conduits, and squares all over Moscow were restored. Czar Nicholas I commissioned Constantin Thon to build the Grand Palace of the Kremlin in the 1840s to lodge the imperial family when they visited Moscow. This massive, two-story building was filled with enormous apartments and halls. The elaborate Hall of St. George contained marble plaques honoring military heroes. The Hall of St. Vladimir connected the palace to the Terem. Thon also built the Church of the Redeemer within the Kremlin walls.

A revered collection of national treasures was moved into the Oruzheinaya Palata, an armory constructed by Thon in 1851. It contains weapons, armor, gold and silver objects, jewelry, vestments, thrones, crowns, costumes, harnesses, and carriages collected by the imperial family since the twelfth century. Among the treasures can be found the helmet belonging to Alexander Nevsky's father; the golden throne of Boris Godunov set with pearls, rubies, and turquoise; and the throne of Alexis Romanov studded with more than eight hundred diamonds.

As a fortress for the aristocracy, the

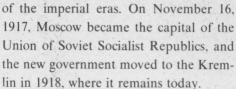

The Kremlin was one of the focal points of the Russian Revolution. Above, czarist officer-cadets guarding the walls of the Kremlin in 1917.

Below, an early parade at the foot of Lenin's tomb. Such ceremonies are a frequent sight in Moscow.

Kremlin guarded the last of the forces resisting the Russian Revolution in 1917. The new spirit brought by the Revolution gave renewed meaning to the architecture of the imperial eras. On November 16, 1917, Moscow became the capital of the Union of Soviet Socialist Republics, and the new government moved to the Kremlin in 1918, where it remains today.

Soon enormous red star-shaped lights were added to the spires of many of the Kremlin towers, filling the city with the light of the Revolution. Half of the churches were demolished in the first wave of Communist Russia's renunciation of religion. The function of many of the remaining churches was radically altered to fulfill the demands of the new regime. The churches of the Kremlin became museums. The objects they preserve, as well as the architecture itself, symbolize centuries of czarist rule in Russia and are a reminder of the long history of increasing subjugation of the Russian people by the aristocracy.

In the 1930s, a major structure was added to Red Square. A large, mastaba-like pyramid was built of red granite and black and gray feldspar by the architect Shchuzev to hold the embalmed corpse of Lenin (Vladimir Ilyich Ulyanov), the founder of new Soviet State. Lenin's body is in clear view within this tomb alongside the Kremlin wall and is seen by thousands of visitors each day. Joseph Stalin's body was housed in the tomb from 1953 to 1961, when it was transferred to a nearby grave.

Under Stalin, there had been other additions to the Kremlin, but none as prominent as Nikita Khrushchev's Palace of Congresses—an almost American structure that seems oddly out of place in the Kremlin.

The whole history of Russia can be read in the architecture of the Kremlin. The site that was once a small wooden fort on a knoll overlooking the Moscow River is now the bastion of the Union of Soviet Socialist Republics, surrounded by buildings attesting to the fallen majesty of imperial Russia.

Wawel Castle,

Poland

Preceding page, the Wawel seen from the southwest. Remains of the ancient Gothic castle are visible at the base of the royal palace. Beyond, Wawel Cathedral.

Above, the east side of the royal palace. Foreground, the Gothic pavilion with its elongated buttresses. Also visible is a Renaissance belvedere, a roofed gallery built upon the former ramparts.

Below left, the great arcaded courtyard, the work of Francesco Fiorentino and Bartolomeo Berecci.

Below right, the courtyard of the palace seen from the loggias on the eastern side.

Facing page, the western façade of the courtyard. The splendid windows designed by Francesco Fiorentino are decorated with the arms of Poland, Lithuania, and Austria.

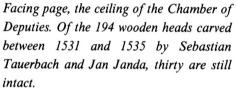

Facing page, the ceiling of the Chamber of Deputies. Of the 194 wooden heads carved between 1531 and 1535 by Sebastian Tauerbach and Jan Janda, thirty are still intact.

Above left, "Man in a Princely Hat," one of the carved heads on the ceiling of the Chamber of Deputies.

The Senate Chamber (above right) is hung with magnificent Flemish tapestries illustrating the story of Noah.

Center, Flemish tapestries from the collection of King Sigismund Augustus which decorate the Chamber of Deputies.

Below right, the bedchamber of Sigismund I, furnished in the style of the early sixteenth century.

Above left, the sarcophagi of the Polish kings and national heroes beneath the Romanesque vaults of the crypt of St. Leonard, part of the second cathedral. Far left, a Romanesque capital, from the church later replaced by the present Gothic building.

Left, the pre-Romanesque chapel, built in the eleventh century.

Above, the Gothic room named after King Casimir the Great. Dating back to the mid-fourteenth century, it became the official treasury during the sixteenth century.

Left, the Notched Sword is the most sacred relic of the ancient Polish royalty. It is exhibited in the Hall of Hedvige and Ladislaus Jagiello.

Above left, the Renaissance interior of the Chapel of Sigismund, showing the tombs of Sigismund I, Sigismund Augustus, and Anna Jagiello, carved by Italian artists.

Above, the sheaf, emblem of the Vasa dynasty, combined with the Polish eagle on a seventeenth-century shield.

Below left, the tomb of Casimir the Great, under whose rule Poland flourished.

Facing page, the mausoleum of St. Stanislaus, the patron saint of Poland. The baroque structures designed by Giovanni Trevano are incorporated into the severe Gothic interior of the cathedral.

Following page, a view of the cathedral from above. Polish kings were both crowned and buried in the cathedral at Wawel.

Wawel Castle, Poland

According to a Polish legend of the Middle Ages, a ferocious dragon lived in a cave on a hill called the Wawel, overlooking the Vistula River. During the reign of Prince Krak, the dragon frightened the townspeople into supplying him with tender young animals to keep him from devouring local children. Finally, two sons of Prince Krak slayed the dragon after an arduous fight, liberating the region from the monster.

Once freed from the threat of the dragon, the village prospered and expanded, eventually becoming the city of Krakow. Some two hundred years after the demise of the legendary dragon, the Wawel had become known both for its royal palace and the church where the coronation of Polish kings took place. The burgeoning Polish nation was wealthy, and the monarchy made sure that the castle and church at Krakow were extravagantly decorated. Foreign artists and architects, many from Italy, were commissioned to construct churches and design palace interiors that would reflect the styles currently fashionable in Western European capitals.

The Legend that Grew into a City

Even today, the Wawel dominates the city of Krakow. The legendary dragon's cave overlooks the Vistula from the eastern side of the hill. The remains of the village that once stood on the Wawel can still be seen on the western side of the hill. The original castle and cathedral at Krakow remain intact on the fairly flat top of the Wawel.

The present cathedral at the Wawel is the third reconstruction. The original was a chapel with four vaults built in 1020 during the reign of Boleslas the Brave, who was responsible for making Krakow a significant political, military, and religious center. The second church was partially built on the foundations of the original chapel between 1090 and 1142. The architect Ladislaus Herman erected a Romanesque church which included a crypt built into the hill. A Gothic renovation carried on between 1320 and 1364 resulted in the construction of a typical Central European basilica with a central transept and a squared apse.

During the first half of the sixteenth century, King Sigismund I (1506–1548) commissioned the Florentine architect Bartolomeo Berecci to add a funeral chapel to the Gothic cathedral. Taking an active interest in the project, Sigismund ordered the finest Hungarian marble to be used throughout the chapel. He justified the expense, and it must have been sizable, by saying:

> However much we may lay out on temporal buildings, we shall be ill advised to economize on that, in which we shall abide forever.

Berecci razed a chapel on the south side of the cathedral to make room for the new

Left, the legendary Prince Krak, after whom the city of Krakow was named.

Right, the turreted castle of the Wawel dominates Krakow in this fifteenth-century engraving by Hermann Schedel.

CRACOVIA

houses, and churches were built during this era of prosperity, and by the mid-sixteenth century, Krakow had become a thriving commercial and cultural center.

The blossoming of the Renaissance in the sixteenth century led many Italian architects to foreign capitals where they designed buildings as far away as Fontainebleau and Moscow, thus spreading Renaissance tastes throughout Europe. In Poland, specifically at the Wawel, local masons and architects learned new skills and building techniques from the Italians who supervised the construction of palaces, churches, and monuments. In addition, Italian painters and sculptors proved to be important influences on Polish art, and their works decorated the interiors of the palaces and churches.

The legendary dragon (above left) that haunted the Wawel was slain by the sons of Prince Krak.

Above right, Sigismund III, who transferred the capital of Poland from Krakow to Warsaw in 1609.

chapel, which he modeled after the theories of the celebrated Renaissance architect Leon Battista Alberti. Completed around 1533, the Sigismund Chapel was destined to become a royal mausoleum containing the tombs of Polish kings and the relics of saints.

Wawel Castle was built by Francesco Fiorentino between 1507 and 1536. The design was simple. A large central courtyard was surrounded by four graceful arcades, each three stories tall. This was one of the first courtyards north of the Alps to use Renaissance arcades. The open area was used for official ceremonies, banquets, and jousting tournaments. The Italian design was altered to accommodate the ceremonial and royal functions of the Polish castle. Although the arcades on the first two stories were proportioned according to the Italian model, the arcade on the top story was twice as tall. The columns on the top floor, therefore, were doubled in height; the diameter and distance between columns followed the pattern found on the two lower floors. The taller columns were constructed from two columns—the capital of the bottom column was replaced by a carved stone band onto which the top column was fitted. This departure from the rules of classical taste was designed to provide more light to the rooms under the eaves, imparting a graceful, stately feeling to the courtyard.

The Renaissance at Krakow

One architectural attraction of Wawel Castle lies in the way it blends Italian artistic theories with Polish traditions and techniques. It was not unusual that the Polish castle was built by an Italian rather than a local architect, and the castle contributed to the transformation of Krakow into a Renaissance city. Following the unification of the Polish provinces in the thirteenth century, cultural activity was actively encouraged by the aristocracy at the Wawel, and contributions from France, Italy, Germany, and Bohemia were welcomed. A town hall, markets, the Jagiellonian University, middle-class

Center left, Sigismund I, who began the reconstruction of the Wawel.

Center right, Sigismund Augustus, the great Jagiello king. During his reign, the Wawel reached the peak of its splendor.

Above, the eagle bearing the medallions of the kings of Poland, a sixteenth-century engraving on parchment by Thomas Treter.

The effects of having tailored Italian Renaissance theories to an already existing Polish Gothic fortress are also reflected in the contributions of the four blocks surrounding the courtyard. Only three of the blocks actually housed palace

Palacia S.R.Ma.tis

S. Stanislai

S. Michaelis

Curia Pontificis

Templum Bernardinorum

rooms. The fourth, at the southern end of the palace, was purely decorative and contained nothing more than an attic. This novel concept, originating at Wawel Castle, was later used in Polish castles and palaces built in the sixteenth and seventeenth centuries.

The Wawel—Opulence and Utility

The interior of the palace was richly decorated with paintings, tapestries, coffered or paneled ceilings, carved woodwork, and colorfully tiled stoves. The most opulent examples of decoration are found in the Chamber of Deputies and the Chamber of Senators on the second floor. Particularly striking are the carved wooden heads mounted on the ceiling of the Chamber of Deputies. Of the original 194, thirty remain, all of which are remarkably expressive portrayals of both allegorical characters and contemporary historical figures. According to a legend dating from the sixteenth century, King Sigismund Augustus was about to issue a judgment in the Chamber of Deputies when he was stopped by a voice from one of these heads which warned, *"Rex Auguste, judica juste!"* ("King August, be just!")

The walls of the Chamber of Senators are lined with enormous tapestries recounting the story of Noah. They form part of a collection of 140 tapestries

Above, the Wawel is clearly recognizable in this seventeenth-century engraving on parchment.

bought by Sigismund Augustus. Designed for the Wawel and embroidered in gold and silk thread, they were woven in Brussels by Flemish artisans. The court sculptor, Benedykt, carved wooden cornices over the doorways throughout the palace in a style influenced by Gothic and Renaissance art. Within the Renaissance castle are traces of the earlier Gothic structure. The Gothic pavilion, once called the

"Hen's Foot," projects out from the palace's east wing, supported by graceful buttresses in the Gothic manner.

The fortifications around the Wawel reflect changing architectural styles as well as evolving political developments. Three towers constructed during the fourteenth century remain alongside an outer wall that dates from the sixteenth century. In the next century, an outer bastion was added, which now serves as the base for an equestrian statue of Thaddeus Kosciusko, the Polish national hero known as a champion of liberty. In the late eighteenth century, Kosciusko (inspired by the American Revolution) led an unsuccessful, although courageous, rebellion against the Russian puppet government of Stanislas Poniatowski. Later, after the second partition of Poland in 1793, the Austrian occupying forces added star-shaped forts to the outer walls to prevent further popular uprisings.

A Monument to History

The history of the cathedral and palace at the Wawel mirrors the growth, golden era, and changing national consciousness of the Polish nation. In the tenth century, under Boleslas the Brave, the country expanded and entered an era of prosperity. The Wawel—constructed originally in the Middle Ages and renovated during its Gothic period—entered its most glorious age in the sixteenth century. With the marriage of King Sigismund and his Italian bride Bona Sforza, Poland was introduced to the culture and humanistic philosophy of the Renaissance. The design of the Wawel reveals a harmonious synthesis of Italian and Polish techniques as well as attitudes.

Art and diplomacy flourished at the Wawel until 1596, when Sigismund III transferred the capital from Krakow to Warsaw. Subsequently, the fortunes of the Wawel declined—as did those of the Polish kingdom. In 1795, it was garrisoned by foreign troops, the first of several such disruptive occupations.

This century has occasioned new-found interest in the Wawel. The castle has been restored as a museum and now houses the treasures of past monarchs. There is, in particular, a fine collection of arms, armor, and trophies from the old royal armories: ornate helmets, breastplates, decorated ceremonial shields, even a seventeenth-century Turkish war tent.

Today, the castle and cathedral on the hill are a rightful monument to the history of the Poles and a testimony to the dreams and achievements of earlier centuries.

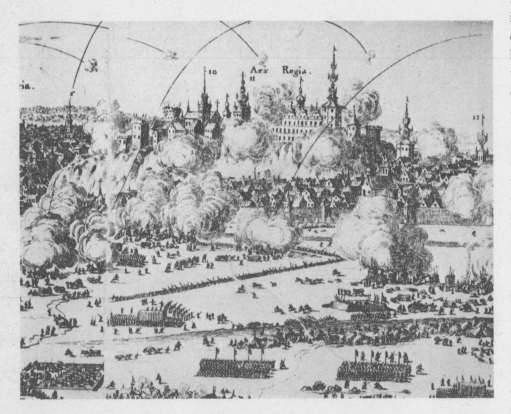

Above left, a view of the fortified palace of the Wawel during the Swedish siege of 1655.

Left, a nineteenth-century drawing by Micha Stachowicz that depicts members of the senate paying homage to Sigismund III in the Chamber of Deputies.

The Tower of London,

England

Preceding page, an aerial photograph showing the succession of walls that once made the Tower of London the mightiest fortress in England. In the middle is the White Tower, the Norman keep built by William the Conqueror. The tower is surrounded by an inner circle of walls, with towers overlooking the outer walls. The bridge (upper left) between the Guard Tower and the Middle Tower was used to cross the moat, which is now filled in.

In spite of a number of alterations, the severe medieval appearance of the Tower has been preserved over the centuries. The coping on the Guard Tower (left) as well as the arched windows (facing page and top left) and doors (above) in the White Tower were added by Sir Christopher Wren in the seventeenth century.

Above left, the Martin Tower, first built by Henry III, which for two hundred years housed the crown jewels and the royal wardrobe.

Below left, the Queen's House, where Elizabeth I ate when she was imprisoned in the Tower. The Queen's House was built during her father's reign. Elizabeth's mother, Anne Boleyn, had been imprisoned in the same building.

The medieval Cradle Tower (above right) dates from the time of the Plantagenets when the Tower was at the height of its glory.

Below right, the Traitors' Gate. At one time, it opened directly onto the Thames as did the door at the base of the Cradle Tower.

Left, the Romanesque Chapel of St. John. Built around 1080, the simple but beautiful chapel occupies part of two stories in the White Tower. The austere stone arches and pilastered columns, which form a colonnaded aisle around the nave, contribute to its aesthetic appeal. From the beginning, the chapel has been associated with the knights of the Order of the Bath, named for the ritual bath taken in the adjoining sword room by men about to be invested into the order.

Above right and center, rooms furnished in the styles of the time when the Tower was last used as a royal residence.

Below right, the Royal Armoury, a museum containing the armor of Tudor and Stuart kings.

The Tower was used as a residence, arsenal, fortress, and prison for the kings of England. Reminders of the vital history of the Tower can be found in the decoration and architecture of the building: the royal coat of arms (above left); the narrow passageway (below left) in the White Tower, more suitable for a fortress than for a palace; and the staircase (below) where, according to legend, Richard III had the bodies of his young nephews buried after he had ordered them murdered.

Above, the Bloody Tower, once called the Garden Tower because it overlooked the garden of the constable of the Tower of London. Its name was changed in the sixteenth century when many were led to believe that the young princes of York had been murdered there. Its portcullis (below right), a suspended grille lowered to protect the Tower from attack, weighs two tons and is the only one in England still in working order. Before it was fitted with winches and pulleys by the duke of Wellington in 1848, it took thirty men to raise.

Above right, the Dudley coat of arms carved in Beauchamp Tower during the imprisonment of the Dudley brothers.

Following page, the Tower at night.

The Tower of London, England

"Much suspected of me, nothing proved can be." It is said that Elizabeth I, the last of the Tudor line, composed these famous words while she was imprisoned in the Tower of London, where she had been sent on Palm Sunday in 1554. Despite her confident tone, Elizabeth was in fact far from certain that she would escape the fate of her mother, who had been decapitated on Tower Green eighteen years earlier after watching her own brother suffer the same fate.

As it turned out, Elizabeth left the Tower unharmed just two months after having entered through the Traitors' Gate, the grim portcullised entrance on the Thames that in itself seemed to pronounce final judgment on untried prisoners. Elizabeth was undoubtedly aware of this when she requested that she be allowed to enter the Tower by another gate.

Elizabeth's release from the dreaded prison was true to the English tradition that kings, queens, or claimants to the throne were eliminated after—not before—they had been virtually excluded from competition for the royal crown. To lose one's head in the Tower of London or in some remote castle was usually not so much a means of preventing possible victory as it was a fate reserved for losers who might be tempted to retaliate. This was true in the case of Edward II, who was deposed by his wife Queen Isabella and her paramour Mortimer and later strangled in Berkeley Castle with a silk cord (or, according to another version, impaled on a red-hot poker). Henry VI, who was crowned king of England and France while still a child and imprisoned in the Tower of London after the Battle of Tewkesbury, met his miserable fate while at his prayers in a small chapel. Richard II—defeated in battle, deposed, and imprisoned by his cousin Henry Bolingbroke—was quietly dispatched at Pontefract Castle.

Only a short time before Elizabeth was taken to the Tower, her sister Mary (who had not yet fully earned her nickname "Bloody Mary") beheaded Lady Jane Grey, the Nine Days' Queen. It had not been hard to dethrone the aspiring mon-

Left, a fifteenth-century manuscript—probably the oldest known illustration of London—from a book of verses compiled and partly composed by Charles Duc d'Orleans (ca. 1415–1440).

Below, the Tower in a print of the mid-eighteenth century.

Below left, William the Conqueror, as depicted in the Bayeux Tapestry, who laid the foundations of the Tower in 1078.

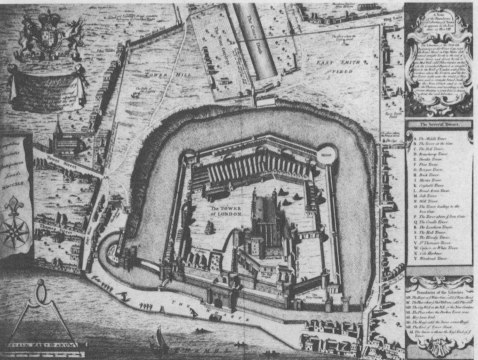

arch, and she passed quickly from the royal apartments to the cells and ultimately to the block on Tower Green.

Though Lady Jane Grey had trembled when she first wore the crown, she died with fortitude. Not even the sight of the tortures inflicted on her husband managed to shake her—the husband who carved her name on the walls of Beauchamp Tower where he awaited the appointed hour of his death. Mary was also responsible for Elizabeth's stay in the Tower. But Elizabeth had her revenge, because as queen she imprisoned many Catholics and later executed her long-time rival Mary Queen of Scots.

The Tower of London is best known as a prison, and its list of famous captives recalls the history of medieval Europe. The great and the infamous—kings, queens, archbishops, abbots, heretics, saints, trai-

tors, and mountebanks—have been imprisoned within the Tower's walls. Some were held for ransom. The less fortunate were beheaded, poisoned, or murdered in mysterious ways. Many prisoners did not leave the Tower even after death but were buried next to one another in the Chapel of St. Peter ad Vincula, occasionally to be joined in time by their persecutors.

One of the most chilling histories connected with the Tower is the mystery of the sons of Edward IV who were held captive there. The two princes were ten and thirteen years old when Edward IV died in 1483. The elder son was crowned King Edward V, but he was soon deposed for being illegitimate. According to a claim voiced by an obscure bishop named Robert Stillington and confirmed by Parliament, his father had been a bigamist. The princes' disappearance made it possible for their ambitious uncle, Richard of

Gloucester, to become King Richard III. In the next century, Shakespeare, in his tragedy *Richard III*, popularized the notion, previously put forth by Sir Thomas More, that the two princes had been murdered at Richard's command.

This tradition denies Richard III a hearing at the tribunal of history. Later research suggests that More, a Tudor supporter who had not been alive at the time of the incident, may have accepted unquestioningly the prejudiced account of Cardinal Morton, archbishop of Canterbury, who wrote the original Latin version of the *History of Richard III*. Morton wished to justify the defeat of Richard by Henry Tudor, later Henry VII, at Bosworth Field. A more objective reading of the evidence suggests that Richard had been a loyal subject of his brother, Edward IV, and had been an earnest and hardworking king in his own right.

Above, left to right: Henry VIII, who ordered two of his six wives beheaded in the Tower; Anne Boleyn, Henry's second wife, who was executed on May 18, 1536; a Hogarth engraving of Lord Lovat, a Scottish patriot and the last English prisoner to be beheaded.

Left, the beheading of Lady Jane Grey, the Nine Days' Queen, who was sent to the scaffold by Queen Mary.

An Architectural Perspective

The Tower of London is an architectural archive of English history. The Roman walls still visible within the outer walls of the Tower are among the few such ancient remains in London, dating from the time that Britain had been overrun by the legions of Claudius. After the Battle of Hastings in 1066, when William of Normandy defeated the Anglo-Saxons and became William the Conqueror, he erected fortifications on the east side of the city to insure his control over the port of London. The Tower, begun in 1078, was designed to protect the Normans from attack. Built of white limestone imported from Caen, France, it became known as the White Tower. The epithet became even more appropriate when the Tower was whitewashed. By the time the whitewash had worn off, during the reign of Henry III, the Tower had become a frightening symbol—many viewers, seeing the limestone structure with its original mortar made from old red Roman brick, were certain that the stones of the Tower had been cemented with blood.

A. Doctor Vther, Lord Primate of Ireland,
B the Sherifes of London,
C the Earle of Strafford,
D his kindred and Friends.

The execution of the earl of Strafford, Charles I's chief minister, in 1641.

The Tower had two functions. It was first and foremost an instrument of war, a deterrent against the independent tendencies of the Anglo-Saxon citizens of London, hostile to the Norman monarchy. It was also a royal residence. In the late eleventh century, a new building replaced William the Conqueror's temporary wooden fort. Although on a grander scale and more complex, the new Tower was essentially typical of the familiar Norman feudal keep or fortified manor, a combination residence, fortress, and renowned seat of government.

The principal architect, Bishop Gundulf, was a priest from Rouen. Because of Gundulf's architectural contributions, William the Conqueror made him the administrator of Canterbury and later bishop of Rochester. Gundulf's Tower of London is roughly a cubic block. The base is 106 feet by 117 feet, and the tower itself is 88 feet high. Rising above the keep at each corner are four turrets: three square and one round.

At the southeast corner, a projecting semicircular bastion contains the apse of the Chapel of St. John, the oldest church in London. Its austere, simple Norman interior is considered to be one of the finest rooms in the Tower complex. It was in this chapel that the knights of the Order of the Bath were received into their select society. In dungeons beneath the chapel, prisoners were frequently tortured without trial or reprieve. Although the dungeons were initially subordinate to the royal residence and watchtowers, the Tower of London eventually became the most famous prison in England. It symbolized all the fear and uncertainty associated with the potentially capricious rule of an absolute monarch.

By coincidence, the first prisoner, Rannulf Flambard, happened to be the first to escape from the Tower. He was the second architect of the Tower as well as bishop of Durham and prime minister to William's son, William Rufus. Arrogant and unscrupulous, he abused his office by selling church appointments to the highest bidder and was ultimately imprisoned for acts of extortion. He escaped from the White Tower, after having first made sure his guards were in a drunken sleep, by sliding down a rope of knotted sheets and diving into the moat. His careful plan had not, however, allowed for the Tower's windows, and it was only with great difficulty that he managed to force his enormous girth through the opening. Badly bruised, he fled to Normandy and participated in an unsuccessful invasion of England by Robert, duke of Normandy.

Such an escape was relatively easy at the time, since the Tower stood alone on Tower Hill. However, beginning in the reign of Richard I, the Tower was surrounded by an imposing system of concentric fortifications, making escape exceedingly difficult. The only access to the Tower from dry land was by way of the

Those who entered the Tower through the Traitors' Gate (above right) rarely saw the outside world again. Prisoners were either executed or jailed for years in one of the towers (above left).

Left, a message scratched in the Broad Arrow Tower by a Catholic prisoner.

bridge at the southwest corner, an entrance which was fortified by massive, defensive structures.

The crown jewels, dating chiefly from the times of the Stuarts, the Hanovers, and the Windsors, are one of the greatest attractions at the Tower of London today. During World War II, the precious jewels were secretly moved to an even safer place than the old English fortress. The Tower was at this time virtually empty except for the imprisoned Rudolph Hess, Hitler's lieutenant who had flown to England to propose an unauthorized peace plan.

Hess was lodged in the Queen's House, where Elizabeth had dined during her visit to the Tower. Hess was the last of a long line of prisoners, notable among them were Anne Boleyn, Sir Thomas More, Catherine Howard, and William Penn—the Quaker who later founded Pennsylvania and made it a state that became renowned for its tolerance.

If Hess had gone to the window to look after the flowers in the box, he would have seen the Bloody Tower to his right. There, Sir Walter Raleigh—courtier, soldier, poet, and founder of Virginia—was imprisoned, as was Sir Thomas Overbury, whose food was spiced with nitric acid and washed down with wine laced with sublimate of mercury. Had Hess looked directly in front of him, he would have seen the Tower Green, where so many noble heads had fallen. There died Lord Hastings as

well as the Countess of Salisbury, who danced so wildly around the block that she disconcerted her executioner. Catherine Howard, on the other hand, spent the night before her execution practicing with a block, so that when the moment of her beheading arrived she would display behavior appropriate to her rank.

From the Queen's House, Hess would have also seen the Union Jack flying above the White Tower. This flag was the symbol of a proud nation that held the Tower of London—a stronghold of unbridled power—as a coveted emblem of national independence as well. The commander of the beefeaters (originally the personal guards of Henry VII and now custodians of the Tower) takes off his splendid Tudor cap every evening at exactly 9:40 and cries, "God Save Queen Elizabeth!" And it is with battle-tested conviction that the ranks—clad in the sumptuous bearskins they wear in honor of their victory over Napoleon's imperial guards at Waterloo—reply, "Amen!"

Palace of Knossos,

Crete

Preceding page, the palace of Knossos after Sir Arthur Evans's excavations and restorations. The area known as Knossos was already inhabited at the beginning of the second millennium B.C.

Above, the foundations of the palace and the partly reconstructed north wall.

Left, the northern entrance with its typical Minoan arcade of columns that taper slightly toward the bottom. The palace was a multilevel conglomeration of buildings whose complexity seems to substantiate the myth of Minos's labyrinth.

Above and below, the loggia and great staircase of the palace reconstructed by Evans. The ancient Cretans used the staircase to connect floors having different plans.

Above left, the "theater." Situated in the northwestern corner of the palace, this is the earliest known theater in the history of Western architecture. In effect, it consists of two large flights of steps of unequal length which meet at right angles, forming an empty space in the resultant L-shape. The theater is possibly the first structure constructed for the sole purpose of allowing spectators to view an event. Below left, the series of courtyards, contributing to the fluid layout of the palace.

Facing page, the so-called "Horns of the Consecration" (above right) which rise against the sky. Their purpose has not been discovered, though they are the most dramatic ruins found at Knossos.

The pattern of the buildings around the great courtyard (below right) can be discerned from Evans's reconstruction, but the elevations of the building are more difficult to imagine as is the nature of the spaces they enclosed.

The classic Minoan column, tapering toward the bottom, is the most distinctive feature of Cretan architecture. The original columns were destroyed by fire or erosion and have been reconstructed by Sir Arthur Evans based on the fragments he discovered at Knossos. The use of columns tapering at the bottom began to fade with the end of the Cretan civilization.

Below, the pithoi, huge Minoan storage jars in which wine, oil, grain, and other food-stuffs were kept at Knossos. Decorated with reliefs imitating the ropes with which they were hauled, the jars were piled upon each other in the great warehouses of the palace. It has been suggested that these huge vessels also contained tributes paid to the king by foreign peoples.

The bull was the sacred beast of the Mino-ans, and the word "minos" is linked etymo-logically to the mythological Minotaur, who was half man and half bull. The various representations of bulls (shown on these pages) reveal the grace with which Minoan artists used rhythm and line in their compo-sitions and frescoes.

Below, far right, fresco of a Cretan woman. This charming fragment was nicknamed "la Parisienne" by the archaeologists who found it. Other frescoes depicting scenes from Knossos, such as the one above, sug-gest that the civilization was less puritanical than the succeeding Greek societies.

Following page, the central courtyard of the palace. Like the market square of a small town, the courtyard was the center of activ-ity at Knossos.

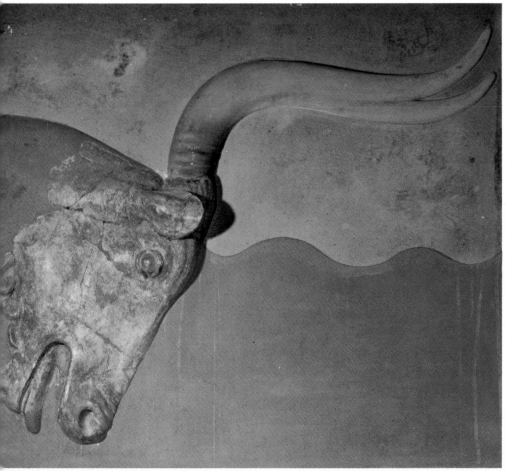

Palace of Knossos, Crete

Myth, history, and legend all converge in the great palace of Knossos. The history of the island of Crete is inseparable from its mythology; tales of gods, heroes, and marvelous creatures are woven into all accounts of Cretan civilization. The palace of Knossos belongs to a fabulous and bygone age, and its mysterious heritage captivates the imagination of visitors to the restored site.

In contrast to the richness of its mythological history, the remains of the palace have furnished archaeologists with little definitive evidence of its past and leave

Below, a cross-sectional drawing made as a result of Evans's excavations. Evans has been accused of being slipshod and unprincipled in his archaeological work, yet he was responsible for the rediscovery of an entire civilization.

many of its mysteries unsolved. It seems likely, however, that the island's civilization gave rise to that of Greece, which in turn had a powerful influence on European culture.

Radiocarbon dating tests have confirmed that a civilization existed at Knossos as early as 6000 B.C. Remains of this Neolithic population were discovered by Sir Arthur Evans, a British journalist and archaeologist who spent much of his life exploring and restoring the ruins at Knossos. By 2000 B.C., there were several palaces on the island of Crete, including the one at Knossos. Earthquakes around 1700 B.C. left all of these palaces in ruins. The palace at Knossos, residence of the king who ruled Crete, was reconstructed and became the center of the civilization that dominated the Aegean during the Bronze Age from 1600 B.C. to 1400 B.C.

The Mythical Past

The story of Minos, the predominant myth of Cretan civilization, exists in many forms. One version states that Minos, king of Knossos, was the son of Zeus and Europa. (However, according to Sir Arthur Evans, "minos" was a title given to the ruler of Knossos, much as Egyptian rulers were called "pharaohs.") Zeus, dis-

guised as a bull, had abducted the maiden Europa and carried her on his back from the mainland to Crete. Minos married Pasiphaë, the daughter of the Sun, who bore three children: Androgeos, Ariadne, and Phaedra. Pasiphaë also gave birth to the Minotaur (a creature with the head of a bull and the body of a man) as a result of her amorous liaison with a bull. Minos hired Daedalus, an exiled Athenian architect and sculptor, to construct a labyrinth to house the Minotaur. Daedalus designed an elaborate labyrinth which was so confusing that, once inside, it was virtually impossible to find a way out. Because the Minotaur's bull–father was sacred to the sea god Poseidon, Minos sacrificed young

Below, Sir Arthur Evans, the English journalist and archaeologist who discovered the palace of Knossos while looking for clay tablets.

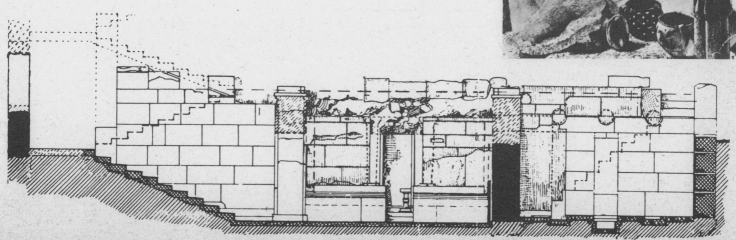

boys and girls to the Minotaur as a means of appealing to Poseidon for protection for his island kingdom.

After the labyrinth was completed, the jealous Minos accused Daedalus of having assisted Ariadne in her plot to help kill the Minotaur. As punishment, the architect was imprisoned in a tower with his son Icarus. Seeking a route to escape from the tower, Daedalus found that Minos guarded all means of access to the sea. Daedalus fashioned large wings out of wax and feathers so that he and Icarus could escape through the air. As the two were flying from the island across the Aegean, Icarus, enraptured and emboldened by his flight, flew too close to the sun. His wings melted, and he plunged to his death in the sea.

Daedalus, however, arrived safely in Sicily. Many years later, Minos visited the king of Sicily and was murdered in his bath by the king's daughters, who poured boiling water over him. Despite his cruelty, Minos had been a just ruler and so became a judge in Hades.

A Mysterious Ruin

In spite of this interweaving of myth and history, on many subjects the stories are strangely silent, and the historical past of Knossos is still a matter of conjecture. No one knows, for example, how the ultimate destruction of the second palace in this capital of 70,000 inhabitants came about. However, what did seem clear to Evans was that the ultimate demolition of the palace must have been sudden. Perhaps it was due to an uprising of the people or an invasion from the mainland of Greece. It could even possibly have been

Above, a tablet inscribed in Linear B, the script which aroused Evans's curiosity in Knossos. Linear B was deciphered in 1952 by Michael Ventris, a British linguist, who found it to be an archaic form of Greek.

Below left, the serpent goddess, one of the most famous works of art in the history of archaeology. The other small votive figures were also excavated at Knossos.

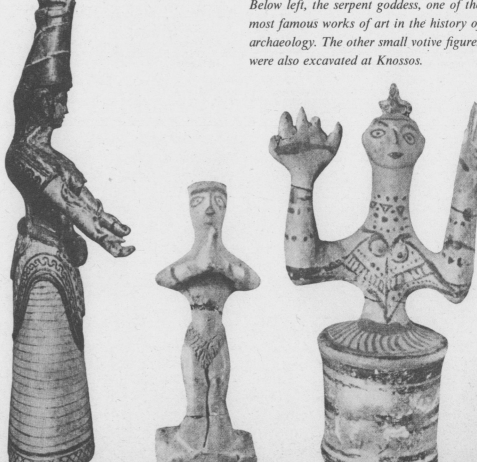

Right, the objects found by Evans at Knossos have been invaluable in reconstructing Cretan culture. Above, a Minoan chessboard.

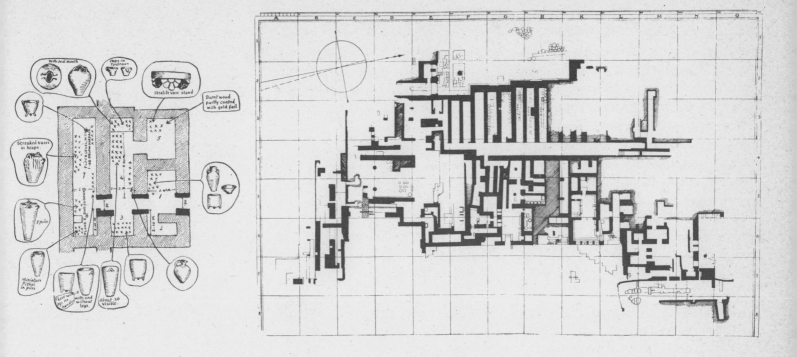

The vast and well-stocked storehouses at Knossos proved that the power of Minos was commercial as well as political.

Above, a diagram of a storehouse and its contents.

Right, a ground plan of the eastern wing of the palace. The long rows of storehouses are adjacent to the central corridor.

caused by another series of earthquakes. Whatever the cause, the era of Minoan prosperity apparently ended abruptly in one night of fire. All that remained were the ruins of the palace—the only clues to an understanding of the civilization of Crete. The palace was never rebuilt; in succeeding centuries only a few poor huts were erected on the site.

The history of Knossos and Cretan civilization was as ambiguous to the ancient Greeks as it is to us. The poet Hesiod, writing in the eighth century B.C., referred to Crete as the land of the gods. Later, writers, historians, and philosophers were inspired by the legends surrounding the island. But by classical times, Crete retained none of its former power.

In the thirteenth century A.D., the redis-

covery of Crete by the Venetians brought the island to the attention of medieval Europe. Some people theorized that the island was in fact the lost continent of Atlantis described by Plato. From the fifteenth century onward, many Europeans traveled to Crete. It was assumed that the few fragments on the ground at Knossos were the only remains of the Minoans.

In 1886, an association was formed in Crete to promote the educational and cultural resources of the island. Archaeological pursuits were encouraged, and further excavation was undertaken by Greeks and Europeans. In 1900, Sir Arthur Evans purchased Knossos from the government of Crete and began to excavate the desolate site. Prior to this, Evans had been a correspondent for the *Manchester Guardian* and also keeper of the Ashmolean Museum in Oxford. Evans hoped he might discover clay tablets at Knossos incised with pictograms, or pictorial symbols, through which he might gain an insight into the language of the early inhabitants of Knossos and thus be able to separate myth from fact. However, Evans's search led him serendipitously to discover the heart of the entire Minoan civilization. The dig, which was to have lasted a year, became his life's work and ultimately earned him a baronetcy.

A Labyrinthian Palace

Within five years, Evans and his team of Muslim and Christian workers had unearthed and restored most of the palace. Built on a hillside on the foundations of earlier palaces, the palace is labyrinthian—a complex of rooms, corridors, porticoes, steps, terraces, cellars, courtyards, chapels, and warehouses that formed a square with sides about 490 feet long. Its builders had mastered that most difficult of architectonic elements, the staircase, and they fully exploited the freedom of space and flexibility of composition which this allowed them—building at times on as many as five levels. Indeed, it is the fluidity and variety of the construction, the alternation of flat surface and colonnade, which give the palace its character.

Among the many distinctive features of the palace are the brightly painted wooden columns which taper toward their bases and the graceful frescoes depicting scenes of Minoan life. These frescoes were pieced together from fragments during Evans's years at Knossos.

The palace was built around a large central courtyard of about 198 feet by 96 feet. On the west side of the courtyard, the palace, which reached three stories in height, housed the official apartments, the throne room, sanctuaries, the treasury, and warehouses where huge jars of oil and foods were stored. On the east side, the Grand Stairway led to the level of the private apartments, the Hall of the Double Ax, workshops, the Queen's Megaron (chambers), and a bathroom where running water was provided by clay pipes. Service rooms and lodgings for servants and guards were located at the north and south ends of the palace.

There were entrances to the palace on the north, south, and west sides. The west entrance was used by merchants and commoners, while more illustrious guests entered at the north. Since Knossos was unchallenged in its control of the island and the surrounding sea, the palace had no need for elaborate fortification, and sentries stationed at the entrances to the palace provided the only defenses.

An important feature of the palace is the open-air theater, a large rectangle with a capacity for at least five hundred spectators. West of the theater lay the Little Palace and the Royal Villa, which were used as private residences by the king after the main palace was destroyed somewhere around 1400 B.C.

The Enigma Endures

Sir Arthur Evans had no doubts that his archaeological findings gave historical credence to ancient mythology. He wrote:

We know now that the old traditions were true. We have before us a wondrous spectacle—the resurgence, namely, of a civilization twice as old as that of Hellas. It is true that on the old Palace site what we see are only the ruins of ruins, but the whole is still inspired with Minos's spirit of order and organization and the free and natural art of the great architect Daedalus.

Evans's discoveries and restorations at Knossos have provided the modern world with an intriguing view of Cretan civilization where young men and women apparently did acrobatic feats on the backs of bulls. Knossos was certainly the capital of the wealthy mercantile empire of Crete, strategically located at the intersection of the major trade routes between Europe and the Middle East during the Bronze Age. Yet, the kingdom which flourished at Knossos vanished mysteriously, and even after Evans's extensive findings, the mystery is still unsolved.

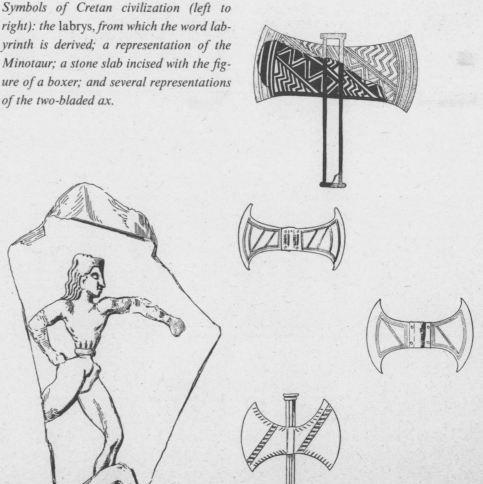

Symbols of Cretan civilization (left to right): the labrys, *from which the word labyrinth is derived; a representation of the Minotaur; a stone slab incised with the figure of a boxer; and several representations of the two-bladed ax.*

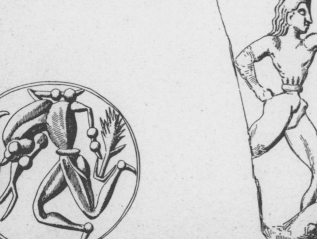

Hradčany Castle,

Czechoslovakia

Preceding page, Hradčany citadel rising above old Prague.

Left, the Gothic Cathedral of St. Vitus, built on the site of the tenth-century Rotunda of St. Vitus, was begun by Charles IV in 1344 but not completed until 1929.

Above, the twelfth-century Basilica of St. George preserves the highest moment of Bohemian Romanesque architecture.

Below, the Chapel of the Holy Cross in the Second Courtyard.

Facing page, the Black Tower, one of the few remaining traces of Hradčany's Romanesque fortifications.

Left, figures of fighting giants which dominate the entrance courtyard. Their exuberant Prague baroque style contrasts with the classical baroque severity of the Hradčany façade, part of an eighteenth-century reconstruction of the castle by Nicolo Pacassi under Empress Maria Theresa.

Center, the Second Courtyard with the projecting Chapel of the Holy Cross.

Below, the tranquil cloister adjoining the Basilica of St. George.

Above, an equestrian statue of St. George and the dragon, a rare fourteenth-century Gothic survival.

Above left, the "crazy" discontinuous late-Gothic net vaulting of the Old Diet Chamber.

Left, the elegant simplicity of the nave of St. Vitus Cathedral.

Above, the almost crypt-like solidity of the Hall of Wenceslas IV in the Old Wing of the castle.

The exuberantly mannered late-Gothic Royal Oratory (facing page) in the Cathedral of St. Vitus appears to be supported in midair by a crown.

Even in this century, new additions of some size and power (above and left) have continued to be added to Hradčany—most notably in the twenties with the work of Josip Plečnik.

Below, the refined delicacy of Central European rococo.

Left, below left, and below right, life-like images of nobles. Above, fourteenth-century crown of King Wenceslas. Below, King Wenceslas as depicted in his chapel (opposite page).

Hradčany Castle, Czechoslovakia

Hradčany Castle has mirrored Bohemian history since the ninth century. Originally a wooden fortress, it has housed a long line of kings whose dynasties maintained a hold over Slavic lands for centuries.

.Prague is at the geographic center of Europe. This strategic location has enabled Czechoslovakia to play a role remarkable for a country with no navy or seacoast. More than a thousand years ago, the Slavs settled in Prague, where two great European trade routes crossed at a ford on the Moldau River. Two citadels, Vyšehrad and Hradčany, were later built on this site to defend the growing commercial center that was to be Prague.

Hradčany fortress was established as the seat of government in the early ninth century when—according to legend—a peasant named Přemysl was chosen to marry the Slavic princess Libusa. One of their descendants, Vaclav I (known in English as Good King Wenceslaus), was a Christian who ruled from 920 to 935. He laid the foundations of the Rotunda of St. Vitus on the site of the present Cathedral of Prague. Murdered by his younger brother Boleslav, Vaclav I was later honored as a saint. He was thought to be the intermediary between God and the Slavs as well as the protector against the encroaching Holy Roman Empire.

Later generations of the Přemysl dynasty greatly expanded the royal enclave on Hradčany Hill. In 973, a Benedictine convent was established at the Basilica of St. George, and a bishop's palace was added, further establishing Prague as a Christian capital. In the eleventh century, the wooden fortress of Hradčany was rebuilt in stone and enlarged for use as a castle. During the same period, the Rotunda of St. Vitus was razed, and a more imposing structure of the same name was built on its site. The completion of the Romanesque cathedral coincided with the coronation of Bratislas II as king of Bohemia. The cathedral was used subsequently as a burial vault by kings of Bohemia. In the twelfth century, the dry stone wall surrounding Hradčany was rebuilt more substantially. In the same century, the Basilica of St. George was expanded on the site of its tenth-century foundations. It is the finest surviving Bohemian Romanesque building.

After four centuries, the lineage that had originated with the famed peasant

Above, Charles IV of Luxemburg, king of Bohemia, one of the greatest sovereigns of Bohemia. It was under his rule that Prague became a great capital city.

Below, Prague at the end of the fifteenth century, dominated by the then fortified Hradčany Castle, as pictured by Hartmann Schedels in the Liber Chronicarum.

Facing page, a view of Hradčany from the banks of the Moldau River.

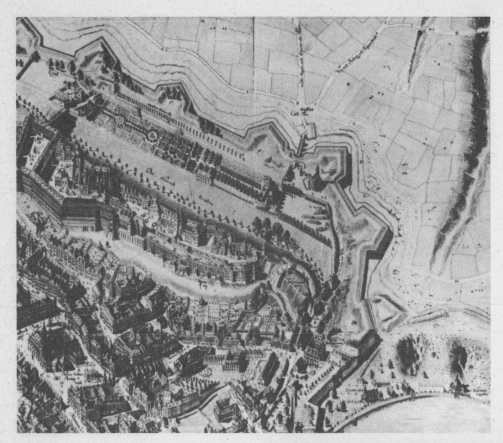

Přemysl finally came to an end. John of Luxemburg, related by marriage to the royal line, inherited the crown in 1306. John valued the Bohemian kingdom primarily for its riches and even sold the ornaments from the tomb of St. Vaclav. Upon John's death, his son Charles became king.

The Golden Era of Prague

The reign of Charles IV, who was elected Holy Roman Emperor in 1355, ushered in the golden era of Prague. By 1373, Charles IV controlled lands stretching from the Danube River all the way to the Baltic Sea, including the present country of Belgium. His architects, Matthew of Arras and Peter Parler, completely rebuilt Hradčany, transforming it into one of the most powerful fortresses in Europe. They also reconstructed the Cathedral of St. Vitus on the foundations of the pre-Christian and pre-Romanesque buildings. At the same time that he was restoring the city's churches, Charles IV founded the University of Prague, which later became the center of the Hussite Movement, a group of followers of the humanist church reformer and martyr, John Huss.

During the reign of his son, Wenceslas IV, sectarian struggles over Communion rituals and the authority of the Bible caused violence and division among the people. Defenestration (throwing people out of windows) became a popular expression of displeasure during this turbulent era.

The successors of Wenceslas were members of the Jagiello dynasty of Poland. Vladislav II Jagiello, the son of the Polish monarch Casimir the Great, ruled from 1471 until 1526. His architect Benedikt Ried from Pistov rebuilt Hradčany. His Vladislav Hall in the castle was one of the largest Gothic secular halls in medieval Europe—although its windows were

Facing page, a drawing (above left) of the reconstruction of the castle carried out under Maria Theresa. Clearly shown at the foot of the hill are the post-Renaissance-type bastions whose cannons protected both palace and city. Above right, a design of 1723 by the celebrated architect Fischer von Erlach for the tomb of a nobleman of Prague. Below, an illustration depicting the 1618 Defenestration of Prague, an act which led to the Thirty Years' War.

Above, two different views of the hill of Hradčany and the suburb of Prague called the Kleinseite, which lies between the hill and the Moldau River.

one of the first examples of Renaissance architecture outside of Italy.

The Jagiellos were succeeded by the German Hapsburg dynasty in 1526 when Ferdinand I became king of Bohemia and Hungary. The Hapsburgs, Catholic sovereigns, had been trying to gain control of Bohemia for centuries. Ferdinand began to create a centralized Catholic state by denying the Bohemians the religious

rights they had fought to gain in previous centuries.

Ferdinand's energies were not restricted to making political and religious changes. He also rebuilt and enlarged Hradčany Castle. The palace now spanned the Stag Moat and contained "Italian" gardens and pavilions in which courtly festivities were held.

In 1567, Ferdinand's successor Maximillian II granted religious equality to the

Czech Estates and Utraquists (a sect that advocated partaking both bread and wine in Communion). The Catholic Hapsburgs grew more tolerant of the Bohemian Protestants during the reign of Rudolph II. His monarchy spanned a period of great cultural and scientific activity. Johannes Kepler and Tycho Brahe made great advances in astronomy. The court painter Giuseppe Arcimboldo and artists of the school of Prague gained respect through-

Above, the entrance to the castle as shown in a nineteenth-century engraving.

Below, another more romantic nineteenth-century view of the ancient fortress as seen from a more picturesque side.

The Hapsburg emperor Ferdinand II was crowned king of Bohemia in 1617. His coronation ended the period of religious tolerance. After the second Defenestration of Prague in 1618, persecuted Protestant Bohemians were forced into exile, and Bohemia lost its independence. The Hapsburgs waged a campaign of Germanization in Bohemia and divided confiscated Czech land among German aristocrats, mercenaries, and Jesuits. Heavy taxes were levied upon the Bohemians by their Hapsburg landlords, and Prague was reduced to a provincial town. Only later, after the Thirty Years' War, were the palaces and churches of Prague rebuilt by the Catholic victors.

out the continent. Hradčany was filled with a great number of archaeological treasures and works of art from Bohemian history, including the ceremonial sacred crown of Bohemia believed to contain a thorn from Christ's crown.

During the reign of the empress Maria Theresa, the architect Nicola Pacassi was largely responsible for reconstructing Hradčany. He superimposed a dull baroque mask over the more picturesque assemblage created by previous monarchs. The oldest part of the castle was surrounded by reconstructed buildings, and the Italian Renaissance gardens were restyled after French baroque models. In the nineteenth century, the gardens were redesigned once again, this time in the English manner.

Today, a visitor to Hradčany can follow the course of Czechoslovakian history by touring the castle. The irregular rectangular shape of the castle reaches from medieval Slavic roots (in its eastern section) to the modern era (in its western section). There is a constant reminder of Bohemian history in Hradčany, as each monarch rebuilt the architecture of his predecessors in a style distinctive to the period. The survival of the castle and cathedral at Hradčany emphasizes the recurrent theme that the architectural creations of sovereigns are more resilient than those of their monarchies.